An Angel's View

Encountering God Through the Stories of the Heavenly Hosts

Michael O'Neal

21st Century Christian Inc.

A portion of the royalties from *An Angel's View* will go to support the precious work of the Mount Dora Children's Home.

Table of Contents

Part 4 Justice of God

Part 5 Sovereignty of God

Acknowledgements

Hidden behind the pages of all books, a unique journey of development occurs. This book came about through the encouragement and guidance of the following, to all of whom I am greatly indebted. A number of years ago my wife stimulated my interest in the topic of angels by suggesting I teach a class on the subject from Edward P. Myers' book, *A Study of Angels*. After teaching numerous classes on the subject, Tom Cain, a member of the Central Church of Christ in Cocoa, Florida, challenged me to make the topic more practical. Even though I worked a few useful insights into the coursework, it still largely consisted of an intellectual study of the angels.

When it was time to select a guided research topic at the Harding University Graduate School of Religion, I really wanted to investigate a research question associated with spiritual formation. Evertt Huffard, the dean of the school and my faculty advisor, knew of my work on angels and suggested I tackle something in that area. Remembering Tom Cain's challenge, the opportunity was before me to come up with a concept that would make the topic of angels more useful to the contemporary Christian. Professor Mark Powell was assigned to supervise my work, and we decided an interesting research topic would be "What Angels Tell Us about God." Upon delving into the subject, it did not take me long to realize that this was a rich topic.

After completing the guided research paper, Professor Powell encouraged me to consider writing a book on the subject. He believed it would have much appeal as a popular work. Twenty-first Century Christian graciously took interest in the topic as a book concept, so I set out to convert an academic work into a book for a popular audience.

I am extremely grateful for the book's reviewers along the way. My wife and son, Steve and Margaret Livermore, Charlie and Gayle Griffin, and Sherri Carlson, all contributed positive yet frank comments that helped make this book a better product. I especially am thankful to Gayle Griffin who tirelessly critiqued this work from a literary standpoint.

Years ago, God placed a passion in my heart to serve Him in a new capacity. He started opening unfamiliar doors that He expected me to enter. God brought individuals into my life to steer me in the right directions. During the creation of this book, constant prayer was offered to God for guidance, so that it would give Him glory, encourage those who read it, and draw them ever closer to Him and His Son. So to my loving God I offer thanksgiving and all the glory.

Part 1

Introduction

Prelude

Getting lost in a good book is a favorite pastime for many of us. The really good ones have an uncanny ability to lure us into their settings and draw us into the lives of the characters. Before we know it, we can be transported from the reality of our physical surroundings into the surreal and vibrant world of the story. If the storyteller is adept at his or her art, we quickly find ourselves caring about the characters and what happens in their lives. The success of retail book stores and on-line book distributors attests to the universal appeal of good stories. Recently, another entertaining activity further reinforced this truth. During our 29-year marriage, my wife and I have enjoyed visiting the city of Saint Augustine, Florida, usually lodging at one of the old bed and breakfast inns there. At some point, we noticed ghost tours were being offered on weekend nights. On our last memorable excursion to the historic city, this eerie enterprise had expanded and numerous tour options had become available. You could go by hearse, tram, bus, sailboat, horse-drawn carriage, or just walk. Whatever your preference, you could be led through some of the supposedly haunted areas of old Saint Augustine, while your guide shared chilling tales. Ready for something besides shopping and museums, I convinced my wife to take one of the walking tours on Saturday night. Hundreds of people were out that night participating in these ghostly tours. I assumed that most people were probably there for the same reason that I was. It was not to catch a glimpse of a ghost; I wanted to hear the stories. I was not disappointed. Dressed for the part, our guide dramatically told riveting legends as we ventured into the eerie settings of cemeteries and spooky old buildings. These were entertaining stories which created lasting memories to appreciate over and over again.

This emphasized the point that good stories have staying power. Some authors and storytellers are especially gifted at engaging our imaginations, bringing to life their characters, building tension, and even causing us to reflect on moral principles. Stories infused with such qualities facilitate our ability to recall even their small nuances years later. Perhaps, in His wisdom, this is why God utilized so many stories in the creation of the Bible. God used narratives to communicate many important matters, such as His character, His enduring love, ethical principles for godly living, sin's consequences, and humanity's frailty and essential need for a savior. And these inspiring stories stamp lasting impressions upon our minds and in our hearts.

It should not surprise us then to see many of the Bible's more momentous stories being underscored by the dramatic. This is where the angels come in. When angels appear in biblical narrative, they immediately grab the attention of the story's characters. The reader's attention is aroused as well. The angels' appearance, powers, messages, actions, and associated visions draw us to God's activity. Something significant is underway, and it will be something to be remembered. When angels enter the picture, God is intervening, and the destiny of His people is often at stake. It was the angel of the Lord who stopped Abraham from sacrificing Isaac, thus preserving the heir of the Israelite nation (Genesis 22:11-12). The angel Gabriel announced to Mary that she would bear the Christ child (Luke 1:26-38). An angel announced to the shepherds that the Savior had been born in Bethlehem (2:9-11). Angels proclaimed Jesus' resurrection at His tomb (Matthew 28:2-7; Luke 24:4-7). To encourage the early church to stay the course, God sent an angel to John, the apostle, to communicate the book of Revelation thus assuring God's people that they will have victory in Jesus (Revelation 1:1; 22:8).

I hope to demonstrate in this book that when biblical narrative involves angels, its purpose is to draw us to God and Jesus. Before diving headfirst into these interesting stories, we need to first come to grips with some of the beliefs associated with angels, and then turn to God's Word to build a reliable foundation for what is true about these heavenly beings.

Chapter 1

Introductory Thoughts

But to which of the angels has He ever said,
"SIT AT MY RIGHT HAND, UNTIL I MAKE YOUR ENEMIES
A FOOTSTOOL FOR YOUR FEET"? (Hebrews 1:13).[1]

Angels are showcased in some of the most captivating stories in the Bible. Shrouded in mystery and accompanied by supernatural powers, angels enter the sphere of humankind to accomplish their God-given missions. And some individuals have even been given a glimpse into their realm. Earthquakes, dazzling light, gates opening on their own, enduring intense heat, blinding of evil perpetrators, shutting the mouths of hungry lions, and striking a king with a deadly affliction are just a few of the spectacular incidents that accompany the stories of the heavenly hosts. When we consider their unearthly power, along with their startling appearance, it is no wonder that people are fascinated with the subject of angels.

A number of years ago my wife asked me to teach a class on angels. With a little prodding on her part, I started to become enthusiastic about the potential for such a class, so I bought several books on angels to thoroughly research the subject. These supernatural heroes of God's Word were right up my alley. For one who is mesmerized by the likes of the X-Men and Spiderman, angels became an intriguing spiritual study for me. Over the years, as I taught several classes on the topic of angels, along with performing graduate-level research on the subject, two issues became apparent to me regarding our culture's rabid interest in angels.

First, what do Americans actually believe concerning angels? The Baylor Institute for Studies of Religion along with the Gallup Organization performed an extensive survey in 2005 on religion in the United States. About 80 percent of Americans polled believed angels either absolutely (61.3 percent) or probably existed (19.2 percent).[2] This surprisingly exceeds the 71 percent who believe Jesus is the Son of God.[3] Even though many religions besides Christianity profess the existence of spiritual beings, I find 80 percent to be a staggering number because of an angel's intangible, spiritual nature. Perhaps this should be viewed as a good thing. Angels are an extensive biblical topic, mentioned more than 400 times, so their recognition should be a matter of faith to those who believe in the authenticity of the Bible. However, closer scrutiny of many contemporary beliefs should raise some concerns.

New Age religion's speculative nature has been a breeding ground for several alarming beliefs regarding our relationship with angels. Examples of some teachings which have their roots based on New Age philosophy are: if something is perplexing you, channel your personal angel to ask him a question; why bother God with your needs, ask angels to fulfill them and assist you in your daily life; if you're not satisfied with your spirituality, seek spiritual growth opportunities with your angel. These perplexing beliefs are not at all based on biblical teachings or facts.

To fuel additional misunderstandings, retail and entertainment outlets offer a wide array of "angel" products that are often very appealing, though not accurate in their depiction of angelic creatures. Most creators of these ceramic figurines, pictures, TV shows, movies, and so forth make little attempt to base their "angels" on biblical data. With the disagreement that abounds concerning much of the above, it is predictable that much confusion surrounds the topic, leaving us to wonder, "What really is an angel?" and "What is our relationship to them?"

The renowned twentieth century theologian Karl Barth believes the caricature of an angel given to us by many artists is so foreign to Scripture that it "does not deserve to be called an angel according to Christian use."[4] Unfortunately, some people in today's culture displace God with these pseudo-angels, but why has this occurred? With all the scandals, quarrels, hypocritical lifestyles, and secular influences that affect so many churches, should we be surprised that people attempt to experience spirituality through other means?[5] Also, if a church's approach to God creates the perception that He is primarily a God of wrath rather than a God of love, it is understandable that some may turn to today's more gentle "angels" for their spiritual solace.[6] Given the fact that angels function as a "means of grace" for many today, perhaps this is pointing us to another key failing in our churches.[7] But this book does not intend to solve the ills that draw people away from the church; rather, it intends to show how the proper treatment of the Bible's angel stories will draw people to God and Christ.

My *second* issue involves how today's angel craze has affected the types of books available in the marketplace. Not only do we have to sort through the many books with all kinds of speculative claims, but many writers who address angelology (the study of angels) from a biblical perspective tend to treat the heavenly hosts as a stand-alone topic. Such items as their nature, attributes, and ministries are evaluated by fitting diverse segments of Scripture together like a jigsaw puzzle. This angel-centered approach promotes an intellectual treatment of the topic at the expense of the spiritual vitality contained within the stories involving the angels. The intent of these stories, and what they should point us to, is sacrificed for a knowledge that ultimately has little practical benefit for the Christian.

I'm not saying that investigating the topic of angels is not a worthy undertaking, because God's Word itself has a great deal to say about them. However, if our main focus is on the angels themselves, we may overlook the ultimate intent of these stories. Angels may momentarily have the spotlight, but the essence of all these stories ultimately has to do with God. The heavenly messengers communicate who He is, His activity in the world, and His desires for His people. If our center of attention is on the angels, it would be kind of like watching a basketball game and focusing on the referees. You may be able to say that you watched the game, but could you identify what player led the team to victory? If we are not careful, our study approach can turn a rich spiritual development opportunity into something shallow.[8] As much as I personally believe in angels, to overemphasize them in one's life and studies could be at the expense of missing God's wondrous work as He pursues a relationship with us.

I believe the purpose of angels will become more apparent if we study the stories involving them with the goal of seeing what is being revealed to us about God and His activity in the world. In the coming pages we will study God's holiness, love, justice, and sovereignty through the lens of the angels' activities. Angels, time and again, will be shown pointing us toward God and away from themselves. Angels will be put in their proper place, as members of God's creation, as agents in the heavenly realm to carry out His will.

Nothing verifies the authenticity of something as well as an eyewitness account. News reporters flood the scene of the day's exciting events to bring firsthand accounts into our living rooms. Slogans like "Eyewitness News at 6" serve to draw us to the program with the "most accurate" news. To develop trustworthy opinions and bring an air of fairness to our judgments, eyewitness information plays an important role in our daily activities. In fact, our nation's judicial system relies on eyewitness testimony to produce fair trials. Being aware of these things, should we not give due consideration to the firsthand account of angels? The angels dwell in the presence of God. Can you imagine what angels must have witnessed – the immeasurable grace, the depths of love, the unfathomable wisdom, the righteous judgments, the creative powers, and the majestic holiness of the universe's sovereign Ruler? Scripture beckons us to better understand our God through the study of these unique eyewitnesses. By observing their responses to God's presence and loyal service to their sovereign Ruler, angels not only serve to enlighten our concept of God, but also provide practical lessons concerning our relationship and responses to Him.

Questions

1. What characteristics do you typically associate with angels?

2. What powers do you typically associate with angels? Can you recall from some of the biblical stories how God puts to use angelic powers?

3. If you followed the New Age beliefs about angels mentioned in this chapter, what concerns would you have for your spiritual development?

4. What are some possible reasons people may turn to angels in their spiritual quests? What should we learn from their actions?

5. Can you recall the various terms that are used for angels in Scripture?

6. Intellectual knowledge of the Scripture is a good thing, but what concerns should we have with an approach to studying the Bible that primarily focuses on gaining knowledge?

7. How do eyewitness accounts factor into your daily decision making?

Chapter 2

Angel Highlights

Bless the LORD, you His angels,
Mighty in strength, who perform His word,
Obeying the voice of His Word! (Psalm 103:20).

Artists over the centuries, and more recently the entertainment industry, have used many concepts to portray angels and their attributes. Close your eyes for a moment and visualize a scene with an angel, complete with supporting cast and props. What does your angel look like? How do you dress your angel? What is this holy one doing? What key features stand out? What are the surroundings? Do any other characters accompany your angel? What influences your picture of the angel?

Since I started researching angels years ago, my wife and I have enjoyed collecting all kinds of angel accessories. We enjoy visiting the Ringling Museum of Art in Sarasota, Florida to see how the artists from the renaissance and baroque periods chose to portray angels. And who could resist checking out how Hollywood depicts them and makes use of their heavenly powers. Not knowing what to believe, all these intriguing portrayals might leave me with the following impressions of angels. From the various forms of artwork I might conclude angels are typically beautiful women; however, the entertainment industry may lead me to believe they are sometimes male. Some angels have a halo of light above their heads, while others just glow in some fashion. Elegant wings are usually a staple characteristic, unless the angel is trying to earn them (remember Clarence from *It's a Wonderful Life*). The angel dress code consists of long flowing garments in white and other soft colors, but current styles may be OK when angels want to blend in with us humans. Playing musical instruments must be a favorite pastime for many angels, while loving on cuddly animals would place a close second. Guarding over us (especially children) seems to be a major angel responsibility. Moreover, I am sure your own culturally-influenced perceptions could easily add to the above.

With such speculative images constantly inundating us, what are we to believe? Before checking out another angel movie, let's turn to God's Word and allow it to accurately shape our view of these mysterious beings. Hopefully, this chapter will clear up several misconceptions and provide a starting point to facilitate our interpretation of the angel stories we will be investigating.

The Bible refers to angelic beings through an abundance of terms. These terms may have dual meanings, so it is important to determine from the context whether a heavenly being was intended by the author. Some of the many names used in Scripture include; angels, archangel, chief princes, cherubim, seraphim, heavenly hosts, hosts, sons of God, watchers, holy ones (saints), and ministers. The archangel Michael and beloved messenger Gabriel are the only angels to be mentioned specifically by name in the Bible. Even though many of these terms are synonymous, some angelic beings appear to be distinct from the others, such as the cherubim and seraphim. We will explore some of their differences, but for the purpose of understanding how they draw us to God and His work, grouping

> The Hebrew and Greek terms commonly translated as angel (*malak* and *aggelos*, resp.) simply mean "messenger." *Aggelos* was used to indicate that John the Baptist was a messenger of God in Mark 1:2. However, in the New Testament *aggelos* typically refers to an angelic being.

them all together into a general class of angelic beings will usually suit our needs.

Have you ever considered that Genesis does not include a creation account for the spiritual realm? Are the angels like God in that they have no beginning or end? Fortunately, the psalmist in Psalm 148 answers this question for us and identifies the angels as created beings. In summoning all creation to praise the Creator, he includes the angels (v. 2) as representatives from the heavenly realm and appeals to them to join the impassioned choruses of praise; "Let them praise the name of the LORD, for He commanded and they were created" (v. 5). Angels are also included in Paul's understanding of what was created; "For by Him all things were created, both in the heavens and on earth" (Colossians 1:16). Scripture is not clear on when angels were created. Yet we learn from Job 38:4-7 that the "sons of God" (angels) witnessed the creation of the earth, which provides our only clue to the timeframe of their creation.

Contrary to the artists' conceptions, angels are never described as being feminine in the Bible, and the terms for angels only appear in the masculine form.[9] Nevertheless, we should recognize they are spirit beings. The writer of Hebrews acknowledges their spiritual nature; "Are they not all ministering spirits, sent out to render service for the sake of those who will inherit salvation?" (Hebrews 1:14). To accomplish their God-given missions, angels have been given the ability to transition from the spiritual to the physical realm. Sometimes they appear as ordinary men (Genesis 19:1-5; Hebrews 13:2). On a few occasions they are referred to as men but are still distinguishable as angels (Acts 1:10; Mark 16:5).

Sometimes angels manifest themselves in a supernatural state as evidenced by the fear invoked by their appearance, and the strange happenings associated with their visitation (Daniel 8:17; 10:4-21; Luke 1:12; 2:9; Acts 10:3-4; Revelation 10:1). Dazzling light often accompanies their descriptions, and like typical good guys, they are often seen wearing white (Matthew 28:3; Luke 24:4; John 20:12; Acts 1:10; Revelation 15:6; 18:1; 19:14). Daniel provided the following description of an angelic being whose extraordinary appearance terrified him, prompting the angel to calm his fears:

Beryl is a precious gem that can be found in shades of yellow, green, and blue. Because Daniel's angel has arms and legs that gleam like bronze, perhaps this beryl is a brilliant translucent yellow. Tumult gives the connotation that the angel's voice was like the roar of multitudes.

I lifted my eyes and looked and behold, there was a certain man dressed in linen, whose waist was girded with a belt of pure gold of Uphaz. His body also was like beryl, his face had the appearance of lightning, his eyes were like flaming torches, his arms and feet like the gleam of polished bronze, and the sound of his words like the sound of a tumult (Daniel 10:5-6).

Wow! Now that would grab our attention! No wonder many became startled, requiring the angels to settle them down. As we will continue to see, the angels of the Bible distance themselves from the soft images perpetrated by mistaken views and false representations.

What about wings? Are wings not the identifying mark of an angel? In angel lore, wings on angels are like stripes on zebras. At least, such is our typical contemporary thought. Case in point; check out the following story.

Preparing Sunday school lessons for first and second graders has always been a cherished activity for my wife. She loves bringing the stories of the Bible into their imaginative worlds. A valuable perk of having a wife who teaches children, is that sometimes she shares their innocent yet intriguing remarks. One Sunday morning after Bible class, she approached me with a smile, anxiously wanting to tell me something. She had an experience that she wanted to share with me from her classroom. That particular

Sunday her lesson had been based on the resurrection of Jesus. To help the children understand this difficult concept, she played an animated account of the resurrection story from a videotape. As the class watched the scene where the women at Jesus' tomb became startled by the sudden appearance of two angels in dazzling apparel (Luke 24:4-5), all of a sudden one of the little boys became frustrated with the angels' appearance and blurted out, "Hey, those aren't angels! They don't have wings." With credit to the video producer, the angels were accurately depicted. However, the boy's understanding of what an angel "should" look like demonstrates how culture had introduced some misconceptions into his perception of angelic appearance. Who knows what may have shaped his concept of an angel? Perhaps it was cartoons, Christmas tree ornaments, or children's books. But this is not just a secular problem; much of children's Christian literature perpetuate misconceptions as well.

I have to confess, I was recently very tempted to use a wing on my company's logo (Angelquake Ministries). My daughter, who is a graphic artist, was creating the artwork for the logo. We both agreed that by incorporating a wing into the logo, everyone would associate it with an angel when viewed in the context of the company's name. As a twinge of guilt crept into my conscience, I realized that I would also be contributing to a questionable teaching. Accountability took hold of my heart, and we chose a starburst of light to use instead.

What can we determine about angel wings from the scriptural depictions? Only the cherubim and seraphim are described as having them (Isaiah 6:2; Ezekiel 1:6-9). Wings are never specifically associated with the "generic" angels of the Bible. If angels truly had wings, how could all the Bible's authors overlook such a prominent and unique feature? Unfortunately though, one of the John's apocalyptic visions may leave us fluttering a bit. Angels are typically depicted as sitting (Matthew 28:2; John 20:12), standing (Acts 1:10; Luke 2:9), walking (Genesis 18:22; 19:1), or riding horses or chariots (2 Kings 2:11-12; Zechariah 1:7-11). However, in Revelation John records that he saw an angel flying in the mid-heaven (Revelation 14:6). Two other angels are said to consecutively follow that one, leaving us with the impression that they too took flight (vv. 8-9). Only in the text of this symbolic book are angels described as flight-worthy (also see discussion of interpretation of Daniel 9:21 in Chapter 7).

Well what about Superman? He does not have wings, yet he can fly. Our modern fictional notions of super beings that fly without wings would have been foreign to John. In fact, John is the sole New Testament author to use this Greek term for "fly," and he only uses it in the book of Revelation. Outside the text in question, all of the other verses are used in association with winged flight (Revelation 4:7; 8:13; 12:14; 19:17). The woman in the vision in Revelation 12:14 is actually given the wings of an eagle, so she can fly into the wilderness to escape Satan's persecution. Along with mythology's use of winged beings, John's idea of flight in the ancient world would have been with wings.

It is important for us to not overlook the symbolism which might lie behind a vision of an angel flying in the midheaven. Like the airplane which pulls a banner to "Eat at Mo's Diner" for those along the beach to see, so is the angel who makes a proclamation from the midheaven, at the pinnacle from which all can see him and hear his message. Therefore, to see an angel flying in the mid-heaven may be purely symbolic to indicate that all will be able to hear his proclamation and may not be intended for us to deduce actual physical attributes of the angel.

Unfortunately, visions are not clear-cut. Sometimes they may only serve to illustrate a concept, while at other times they depict the heavenly realm. Revelation's highly symbolic nature, along with no other biblical evidence of angels having wings, leaves me inclined to believe God's "generic" angels are wingless. However, I have chosen to keep an open mind about the subject because of Revelation 14:6. Perhaps along with the seraphim and cherubim God made other angelic beings with wings. If some angels have the ability to transition to the human realm undetected, is it that far a leap to believe they could adapt to the physical realm of flight? Some day it will be a joy to find out.

Today's depiction of angels with wings has more to do with the artists' imaginations over the centuries than biblical fact. I am sure it was a daunting challenge for the original artists to incorporate a spiritual being into their masterpieces, especially with the limited information the Bible provides of what an angel looks like. It appears the artists adapted some of the ideas used to depict the gods and goddesses of mythology for their portrayal of angels.[10] Consequently, the artistic representations of angels who are beautiful, elegant, winged women had its genesis in mythology and no foundation in biblical truth.

Halos have often been added to the artists' depictions of the heavenly hosts. The origin of this frequently added embellishment also appears to be artistic license and taken from mythology.[11] However, in the Bible it is not unusual to read about an angel emanating light or shining with the brilliance of lightning (Acts 12:7; Matthew 28:3). Ezekiel notes that above the cherubim's heads was "something like an expanse, like the awesome gleam of crystal" (Ezekiel 1:22), but nowhere in Scripture do we encounter the term "halo."

Just as we are servants to our God, angels join us in this privileged occupation. As created beings, they are eager and ready to serve their Maker. God created them as "WINDS" to quickly carry out His will and "FLAMES OF FIRE" to execute His judgments (Hebrews 1:7). The psalmist states, "Bless the LORD, all you His hosts, You who serve Him, doing His will" (Psalm 103:21). Angels consider themselves fellow servants with God's people (Revelation 19:10), but Christians have the unique benefit of being served by them (Hebrews 1:14). Faced daily with the schemes of Satan and spiritual forces of wickedness (Ephesians 6:11-12), is it not encouraging to know that God has spiritual forces of goodness at His disposal? Generally, I would like to persuade each of you to pray for your needs and not for the assistance of angels. However, on one occasion, while in fervent prayer, I asked God to send an angel to protect my best friend's Marine son during the initial stages of conflict in the Iraq war. We have a God who searches the depths of our hearts; He understood my intent. The important thing is to pray, and let God work out how He will answer our requests in accordance with His will.

Some of you might affectionately suggest, "Well, I'm an angel." Of course, how could I stand in judgment of your impeccable, or should we say, angelic behavior? However, if you stated that you would become an angel when you die, I might need to talk with you about what you really believe. This is a common misconception, and I am sure you have seen cartoons where an angel rises up out of the body of a character that has just passed on. A misunderstanding of a statement made by Jesus may also have added to the acceptance of this belief. Not believing in the resurrection, the Sadducees tried to trick Jesus with a hypothetical situation concerning a woman who had multiple legitimate husbands per the Law of Moses. They queried Jesus as to whose wife she would be in the resurrection. Jesus responded by saying, "For in the resurrection they neither marry nor are given in marriage, but are like angels in heaven" (Matthew 22:30). Jesus does not say we become angels, but that we will be similar to them. Like the angels, we will have no need for procreation, as our nature at the resurrection will be eternal.

Scripture bears witness to a few special angelic beings with specific designations. First is the archangel. The term archangel appears only twice in the Bible and means the chief of the angels. Michael is the only angel given this title (Jude 1:9). However, an angel, who was delivering a message from God to Daniel, refers to Michael as "one of the chief princes" (Daniel 10:13), leading one to believe there may be other angels with titles of authority. The Bible does not provide us with the specifics of an angelic order, and I have found most attempts to do so purely speculative. Nevertheless, we find Michael rallying "his" angels to take on Satan and his evil angels, throwing them down to the earth in defeat (Revelation 12:7-9). And at the onset of the End Time, it will be the voice of the archangel who ushers in Christ's glorious return (1 Thessalonians 4:16).

What does the Bible tell us about our second special angelic being, the cute little chubby cherub? Nothing! I'm not sure why so many people think those baby-faced imposters are cute; must be like one's preference between rock n' roll, country, jazz, etc. Whatever the case, these little chubby winged creatures are the artists' portrayals of mythological spirit beings called "putti," but they have also mistakenly been called cherubs. The cherubim of the Bible are not what we would call sweet and huggable.

> The four faces of Ezekiel's cherubim included that of a man, lion, bull, and eagle. Perhaps they were symbolic for the attributes the cherubim possessed; each had the intelligence of a man, ferocity of a lion, strength of a bull, and speed (or vision) of an eagle.

As mankind was driven from God's presence after Adam and Eve ate of the tree of the knowledge of good and evil, cherubim were stationed at the east end of the garden of Eden to prevent any attempted return (Genesis 3:24). Ezekiel positioned these beings at the throne of God (Ezekiel 1:4-25; 10). His description of them is nothing short of bizarre. He stated they had human form, but besides "form" they do not have much in common with us. Each had four faces, four wings, hooves, eyes all over their bodies, and never had to turn as they moved. I am not creative enough to even fashion in my imagination such ominous creatures. Cute chubby cherubs, I don't think so!

To the nation of Israel, God's presence was associated with the ark of the covenant, the tabernacle, and the temple. God spoke with Moses from above the cherubim on the lid (mercy seat) of the ark of the covenant which was placed in the tabernacle's holy of holies (Exodus 25:18-22; Numbers 7:89). This was probably behind the psalmists' declaration that God was "enthroned above the cherubim" (Psalms 80:1; 99:1). The tabernacle's linen curtains and the veil, which partitioned off the holy of holies, were adorned with cherubim, warning of God's presence (Exodus 26:1, 31). Solomon incorporated cherubim on the temple walls and doors as well as erecting two fifteen-feet-high cherubim with outstretched wings in the holy of holies (1 Kings 6:23-36). During a vision, an angel directed Ezekiel to rebuild the temple after Israel's return from Babylonian exile, which included carvings of cherubim (Ezekiel 41:18). And my favorite cherubim reference; David envisions God, as his deliverer, flying on a cherub when coming to his aid (2 Samuel 22:11). If you ever happen to spot a cherub, know for certain that the Almighty is close by.

The third angelic beings with a special designation are the seraphim, which are only mentioned in Isaiah 6. We will take a close look at them in Chapter 3.

Last, an angelic being of prominence in the Old Testament referred to as "the angel of the Lord" is worthy of our attention. The identity of this angel is one of the great mysteries of the Bible and is highly disputed. The leading candidates for the angel of the Lord's identity are: (1) he is a manifestation of God that is used when He appears to humanity; (2) he is the pre-incarnate Christ acting in this role as part of the Godhead; and (3) he is an exalted angel that serves as God's representative. Unfortunately, we do not have the space to do this topic justice, but a little familiarity with it may aid your interpretation of some of the stories we will be entertaining.

What is so prominent about this angel? Scripture often appears to equate the angel of the Lord with God. When Moses encountered the burning bush on Mount Horeb, Exodus 3:2 states that it was the angel of the Lord who appeared to him "in a blazing fire from the midst of a bush," yet verse 4 states that it was God who called to Moses "from the midst of the bush." Who all was in that bush? On another perplexing occasion, the angel of the Lord came to Gideon to commission him to deliver Israel from the Midianites. However, the dialogue appears to use Lord (*Yahweh*) and angel of the Lord interchangeably (Judges 6:11-24). And it was the angel of the Lord who called from heaven, stopping Abraham from sacrificing Isaac and declaring that "you have not withheld

your son, your only son, from Me" (Genesis 22:11-12). Was Abraham not sacrificing Isaac to God? This angel declares the sacrifice
was for him (note the "from me" above). A little presumptuous
even for an exalted angel, is it not?

Some who saw the angel of the Lord believed they had seen
God. Upon Hagar's encounter with the angel of the Lord in the
wilderness, she said "You are a God who sees ... Have I even remained alive here after seeing Him?" (Genesis 16:13). Manoah
and his wife's (Samson's parents) experience with the angel of the
Lord had a similar conclusion (Judges 13:2-23). During their encounter, Manoah did not initially recognize the angel of the Lord
as a heavenly being, but thought he was a praiseworthy man of
God. As Manoah offered a sacrifice to God, the angel of the Lord
"performed wonders" and then "ascended in the flame of the
altar" (vv. 19-20). Oh, to have that on video. Wishes aside, once
Manoah knew that he had seen the angel of the Lord, he said,
"We shall surely die, for we have seen God" (v. 22). Both Hagar
and Samson's parents' fear was appropriate because God Himself stated to Moses, "You cannot see My face, for no man can
see Me and live!" (Exodus 33:20). So, why did they live?

Another peculiar item was that the angel of the Lord accepted
an offering from Gideon (Judges 6:18-21). This was totally contrary to what the revelatory angel exclaimed when John fell at his
feet to worship him; "Do not do that; I am a fellow servant of yours
... worship God" (Revelation 19:10). Along with Scripture equating
the angel of the Lord with God, this makes it troubling to accept
that he is an exalted angel.

The angel of the Lord as a manifestation of God provides an
attractive solution for the above but has one major drawback –
Zechariah treated the angel of the Lord and God as distinct figures. For instance, the angel of the Lord beseeched God on behalf
of Judah during their captivity in Babylon; "Then the angel of the
LORD said, 'O LORD of hosts, how long will You have no compassion for Jerusalem and the cities of Judah, with which You have

been indignant these seventy years?'" (Zechariah 1:12). It seems a little odd for the manifestation of God to be praying to God.

An interesting thing occurred during the angel of the Lord's visit with Manoah. Desiring to honor the angel of the Lord at Samson's birth, Manoah asks him for his name. The angel of the Lord responded, "Why do you ask my name, seeing it is wonderful?" (Judges 13:18). Isaiah prophesied that the coming Savior would also be called Wonderful (Isaiah 9:6). If the pre-incarnate Christ represented the Godhead as the angel of the Lord, the difficulties of the other two options go away. However, Christ's presence in the Old Testament is not free of difficulties, such as it goes against the strong "one God" theme that exists there. God having a tri-une nature is a New Testament concept. John explained that in the beginning Jesus existed with God, was God, and was involved in the creation process (John 1:1-3, 14). Was Jesus then totally uninvolved during the Old Testament era? Perhaps the angel of the Lord was the Old Testament writers' way of expressing a concept that had not yet been revealed. It is worthy of note that "the" angel of the Lord is never mentioned in the New Testament.

> Paul states in 1 Corinthians 10:1-4 that Christ was the spiritual rock which followed the Israelites during the Exodus and wilderness wanderings. Moses tells us that the angel of the Lord was associated with the pillar of cloud that accompanied Israel also during this timeframe (Exodus 14:19).

The angel of the Lord's identity is a topic for which to keep an open mind. I have only provided some of the key points for you to consider for a much more involved discussion. Whatever your opinion is, I think we will still be able to make some valid observations in the stories to come. But we all have our leanings, so perhaps his name is truly *Wonderful*.

Hopefully these angel highlights will prevent us from becoming sidetracked in the coming chapters. Many other concepts concerning the angels will be entertained as we progress, such as their diversity of powers and ministries, as well as the topic of guardian angels. Let us now turn our attention to a God whose holiness is lauded in the heavenly realm.

Questions

1. What concerns should we have with culture's influence on our perception of angels and their purpose?

2. How do angels differ from God? How would you describe their relationship to Him?

3. Why do you think many people were startled by angels? Why were some not startled?

4. Do angels have wings? What is your rationale for your belief?

5. Why do you think God created angels?

6. How would you describe your relationship to angels? Do you find it encouraging that God has them at His disposal?

7. What are the cherubim most associated with in the Bible? What do you think of their appearance?

8. In reviewing the passages on the angel of the Lord, who do you think this heavenly being is? What are some problems with the various options for this "angel"? Is this something we must have a firm grasp on?

Part 2

Holiness of God

Holiness Prelude

Before plunging into an in-depth discussion regarding one of the fundamental attributes of God, let me explain what I mean by the phrase "fundamental attribute." If you asked wives to name the most prominent attributes of their husbands, what would you expect to show up on their lists? Do you think loving spirit, compassion, or willingness to serve would be found? Or perhaps pride, indifference, or an expectation to be served seems more likely? We males may aspire to the former, but in actuality the wives' perceptions may tell the true story. Even though I am having a little fun at the expense of my own kind, the above potential responses from the hypothetical wives point out that our basic attributes describe our character, attitudes, and who we really are deep down inside. These ingrained attributes of the heart in turn serve to drive our behavior. If I am a person with a fundamental attribute of exceptional honesty, you could expect me to be truthful in all circumstances, even if telling the truth could harm me.

God's holiness is one of His most easily recognized fundamental attributes and profoundly shapes who He is. Throughout the Bible, God is referred to as being holy. Isaiah refers to Him as "the Holy One of Israel" (Isaiah 1:4). With great enthusiasm, the psalmist explains that God is worthy of our worship and praise because "Holy is He" (Psalm 99:3-5). Jesus addresses God as "Holy Father" (John 17:11) in His wonderful prayer prior to His betrayal. God also embraces this quality for Himself by declaring that He is "the Holy One in your midst" (Hosea 11:9) and stating directly that "I am holy" (Leviticus 11:44-45).

As should be expected, the rest of the Godhead is proclaimed to be holy as well. Upon Peter's confession of faith in Christ, he stated that Jesus was "the Holy One of God" (John 6:69). During Peter's second sermon, he accuses the Jews that in rejecting Jesus they "disowned the Holy and Righteous One" (Acts 3:14). In a prayer from the apostles, Jesus is referred to as God's "holy servant" (Acts 4:27). Like God, Jesus also identifies Himself as holy. In the letter to Philadelphia (found in the Book of Revelation), Jesus uses the authorial name, "He who is holy" (Revelation 3:7). And with the third member of the Godhead's name being "Holy" Spirit, what more needs to be said?

What does the Bible specifically mean when referring to God as holy? Basically, God's holiness has two dimensions: His separateness and absolute purity.[12] The Hebrew and Greek terms (*qadosh* and *hagios*) carry the connotation of separation. God's separateness comes from His unique nature and position as Creator. As Master Designer of all things, nothing in creation can

> *Transcendence*, when applied to God, is the concept that He is independent and superior to His creation. As such, He is beyond our ability to totally understand Him (see Isaiah 55:8-9).

compare to Him. He transcends it and is distinct from it. Two of His devoted servants illustrate this concept in their words of praise to Him. Moses proclaimed, "Who is like You among the gods, O LORD? Who is like You, majestic in holiness, Awesome in praises, working wonders?" (Exodus 15:11). Hannah prayed, "There is no one holy like the LORD, Indeed there is no one besides You, Nor is there any rock like our God" (1 Samuel 2:2). God's position in all aspects is transcendent to everyone and everything.[13]

The concept of separation extends not only to God's uniqueness and position but also to His moral or ethical holiness. Evil and sin are totally contrary to His nature. God does not participate in sin and is untouched by its degrading power.[14] He is ethically and morally absolutely pure. One of Habakkuk's declarations exemplifies God's ethical holiness; "Your eyes are too pure to approve evil, and You can not look on wickedness with favor" (Habakkuk 1:13). James also states that "God cannot be tempted by evil, and He himself does not tempt anyone" (James 1:13). The perfect moral purity of God's holiness dictates His complete opposition to evil.

The purity of most commodities determines its value. On the Space Shuttle we required two grades of liquid oxygen (LOX). To achieve the desired thrust performance on the main engines, we required propellant grade LOX that was 99.6 percent pure. The Shuttle's fuel cells, which are used to produce electric power, required LOX that was ultra-pure – 99.99 percent. Introducing contaminants to the fuel cells reduces their lives and efficiency. To attain this level of purity, the refining requirements for the LOX increase, as well as its cost. But God's holiness requires no refining. He is already pure – 100 percent holy. Pure goodness!

God's pure holiness creates an ugly predicament for humankind. Because a soul contaminated by the defilement of sin makes us incompatible with our holy God, and because all of us have sinned (Romans 3:23), "Houston, we have a problem." Humankind stands separated from its Creator. The seriousness of this holiness dilemma is revealed in the redeeming sacrifice of Jesus. No act by man could bridge the gulf of this separation. Refining us to remove all contaminants would take an ultimate act by our holy God. Only the cross could yield the purifying blood that would be required to re-establish a relationship with our holy Creator. What a price! What love!

Wherever God is present that place is distinguished as holy. It is not that the place is special; it is because the all-holy One is there.[15] When Moses approached the burning bush on Mount Horeb, the "mountain of God," the Lord told him that he was standing on "holy ground" (Exodus 3:1-5). God met with Moses in the most holy place in the tabernacle, the holy of holies (25:22; 26:34). The temple was also considered holy and the dwelling place of the Lord (1 Kings 8:13; Psalms 27:4; 65:4; 84:1-3; Habakkuk 2:20; Matthew 23:21). If God is present today within the church and individual Christians through the Holy Spirit (1 Corinthians 3:16-17; 6:19-20; 2 Corinthians 6:16-7:1; Ephesians 2:21-22), what implications does that have for us in the context of holiness? In the next two chapters, we will explore how the angels serve to educate us in regard to the holiness of God.

Chapter 3

Angels' Worship and Praise

And all the angels were standing around the throne
and around the elders and the four living creatures;
and they fell on their faces before the throne
and worshiped God (Revelation 7:11).

My wife and I share a love for hiking to the waterfalls of the Blue Ridge Mountains. The call of their grandeur is something we cannot easily resist. We eagerly anticipate the beauty awaiting us as we maneuver along steep trails and switchbacks. Constantly listening for the faint sound of rushing water in the distance, we yearn to start turning hopefulness into reality. The mountains typically hide their watery jewels around heavily wooded and rocky bends covered by dense foliage, so catching an early glimpse of what lies ahead is unlikely. Yet the powerful sound of falling walls of water beckons us onward and steadily divulges we are closing in on our goal. When the trail finally reveals its treasure, the beauty can be so astounding that we have often stood breathless for long moments of time in admiration of the splendor before us. These scenes cause me to reflect on God's supreme creative power and artistic prowess, leading me into profound thankfulness for the beauty God chose to put into His creation.

Many explorers have also been drawn to reflect on God when confronted with nature's majesty. William Reynolds of the United States Exploring Expedition, 1838-42, made the following journal entry concerning his view of the treacherous Drake Passage from a lofty position on Cape Horn at the southern tip of South America:

> We that were so far removed from all that had life, sur-
> rounded with the grand and gloomy wildness of one of Na-
> ture's wildest scenes, felt an utter insignificance. We were awe
> stricken and humbled into fear & wondering, & our thoughts
> turned to the power that made & created all things.[16]

Contemporary Christian singer Steve Green was a personal friend of Rick Husband, commander of the Space Shuttle Columbia that came apart during re-entry. After this tragic accident, Steve appeared on CNN *Connie Chung Tonight* and shared the following thought as he reminisced about an e-mail Rick had sent him during the mission:

> He was looking out the window of the Shuttle, and, in
> fact, said his eyes filled with tears. If there's a story, there's
> a storyteller. If there's a work of art, there's an artist. And
> he marveled at creation and worshiped the creator.[17]

Upon observing the Earth, strategically suspended in the vastness of space, Rick recognized the indelible mark left by a Master Designer upon His creation, and it drove him to tears in a worshipful moment.

Witnessing some of God's more extravagant handiwork has a way of turning us from our own constrained existence to contemplate on who God is and what He has done. As Creator, we recognize that He is totally above and unique from His creation. His power is unparalleled in the universe. Recognition of God's transcendent holiness serves to create awe within us and has a way of driving us to our knees.

Viewing creation is just one way we encounter God's holiness and power. Is this not also possible through His Word and through our experiences while among His holy people? Whatever the case, what should our response be when we are confronted with the realization that we serve a God whose holiness is beyond our comprehension? And ultimately, what are we to expect when someday we behold God firsthand? How does God's Word prepare us for our future encounters with our holy God?

Eyewitness Accounts

During my time at NASA, we went through several improvement initiatives attempting to achieve excellence in our work practices. In doing so, we would often benchmark other government agencies and companies to determine the "best in practice," in order to learn from their experiences on how best to improve ourselves. If we will only pay attention, God's Word provides the same for us. It is steeped with invaluable lessons learned from those who have gone on before us. Their successes and failures will help us navigate the waters of Christian life that are often unfamiliar and turbulent. Being eyewitnesses of God and His holy ways, the angels offer a unique perspective for us to learn from. Perhaps the most instructive passages leading us to understand the depths of God's holiness involve the worship and praise offered by these heavenly beings that have firsthand experience of being in His presence.

Throne Room Visions

Isaiah's throne room vision of God is one of the most impactful stories in the Bible (Isaiah 6). Witnessing God's holiness and glory sets the stage for his call to be God's prophet. Before continuing, I would like to share how an awe-inspiring scene stirred me to turn to God. Throughout much of my career I was privileged to work on the Space Shuttle program. Launches were often around dawn, so a midnight drive through the Kennedy Space Center (KSC) was normal on launch day. This drive became an inspirational time for me. As I approached the Launch Control Center, I could see the Space Shuttle majestically perched on its launch platform. In the pitch black darkness of KSC's wetlands, the launch pad's xenon lights bathed the Shuttle with a pure, bright light. Otherworldly in appearance, it stood as a behemoth, poised to take a cherished few into space. This was like a sacred image to me, driving me into passionate prayer for the astronauts' safety and my vigilance during countdown. Such awe-inspiring images stir our souls and summon us to action.

On a much grander scale, Isaiah's throne room encounter with God would forever change his life. Majestic and in absolute holiness, God was seen sitting on His throne surrounded by the seraphim. Don't be too quick to wish you had been there. For Isaiah the experience was filled with dread: "Woe is me, for I am ruined!" (Isaiah 6:5). At first glance, Isaiah appeared to have recorded much more about the seraphim and their behavior than God. But is this really the case?

> In the year of King Uzziah's death I saw the Lord sitting on a throne, lofty and exalted, with the train of His robe filling the temple. Seraphim stood above Him, each having six wings: with two he covered his face, and with two he covered his feet, and with two he flew. And one called out to another and said, "Holy, Holy, Holy, is the LORD of Hosts, The

Because the Hebrew term for seraphim is used elsewhere for serpents (Numbers 21:6), they may have a serpent-like appearance. Consequently, they may resemble the winged cobra of Egyptian symbolism that adorned royal headdresses and the throne, serving as divine guardians.[18] However, the chief meaning of seraph may be fiery. Thus, the term serpent would be derived from their fiery bite, and the term seraphim is descriptive of their fiery appearance.[19]

Angelic beings are associated with fire throughout Scripture (Hebrews 1:7; 2 Kings 6:17; Daniel 3:24-27; 2 Thessalonians 1:7). Fiery ones also provides a correlation to the fire associated with God's holy presence (Exodus 3:1-5; 13:21; Leviticus 10:1-2; Ezekiel 1:27). Along with their humanlike features, a burning appearance would be the preferred interpretation.

whole earth is full of His glory." And the foundations of the thresholds trembled at the voice of him who called out, while the temple was filling with smoke (vv. 1-4).

In Isaiah's eyes, the seraphim were imposing creatures. They stood above God, had six wings, and flew. Their thunderous voices shook the foundation of the temple, and they could hold hot coals in their hands (Isaiah 6:4, 6). Beings most of us would consider running from and hiding. Yet remarkably, in all their grandeur, the seraphims' otherness only served to emphasize God's majesty and holiness.[20] By themselves, the seraphim too were majestic and holy, but in the presence of the Almighty they took a back seat. These superhuman creatures screened their faces to show humility before their Creator, served as attendants at His throne, and covered their feet in reverence because they stood in the presence of the Most Holy.[21]

Hollywood often casts actors and builds sets that accentuate a star's persona. For instance, Sylvester "Sly" Stallone may only be 5' 9", but when cast with actors similar in height and by reducing the size of the doorframes, Sly appears more threatening. In Isaiah's eyes though, God needs no props. The seraphim's behavior and proclamation tell us that God naturally has no equal.

I am sure you are familiar with family members, friends, or co-workers who constantly try to draw attention to themselves by making claims about their abilities. You should not have to look long and hard to find someone who fits that bill in our society. Even though the seraphim have a legitimate claim to magnificence, their proclamation does not draw attention to themselves but to God. For the seraphim, only God deserves such honor. They enthusiastically let Isa-

> In Hebrew grammar, the repetition of holy three times signifies that God's holiness is supreme and no one is like him. The seraphim confront Isaiah with the declaration that he is in the presence of the all-holy and sole-holy One.[22]

iah know that "He may think they are awesome, but no one, absolutely no one, measures up to God's holiness and glory." God is
their Lord; He is "the Lord of hosts," and no one will walk away from
their presence confused about that.

Undoubtedly this vision left its mark on Isaiah. God's holy nature became a central theme for him upon authoring the book of
Isaiah, referring to God as "the Holy One of Israel" twenty-six
times. Interestingly, Isaiah does not mention the seraphim again.

John recalls a similar throne room scene where "the four living
creatures" also honor God's absolute holy nature, as well as His remarkable might and everlasting existence (Revelation 4).

> And the four living creatures, each one of them having
> six wings, are full of eyes around and within; and day and
> night they do not cease to say, "Holy, holy, holy, is the Lord
> God Almighty, who was and who is and who is to come"
> (v. 8).

In appearance, the living creatures bear some resemblance to
the seraphim in Isaiah 6, as well as to Ezekiel's cherubim in Ezekiel
1 and 10. However, their declaration of God's perfect holiness is
like the seraphim's. As did Isaiah, John brings in view the majestic
nature of the four living creatures, only to have them humble themselves and direct attention to God's holiness and glory. Experiencing God's incredible presence never grows old, as the four living
creatures cannot cease honoring Him with their proclamation.

Let the Worship Flow

Forgive me as I derail us a minute to make some important observations. We'll be back to the throne room shortly. To my cha-
grin, I have noted over the years that several authors believe the
primary role of some angels is to praise God. Not only does that
belittle the angels' worship but inadvertently puts a chink in God's
character. If God designed into His creation an inherent requirement to worship Him, vanity would be an additional attribute of

the Creator that would bear investigation. Nowhere in Scripture do we find God's purpose for creating the angels. We can only surmise some of their functions from the stories in which we find them, so the above reasoning is poor speculation.

Another way to interpret the angels' desire to worship God comes from their firsthand experience; what they witness compels them to worship Him as opposed to being created for it. As Rick Husband's encounter with creation from space drove him to worship its Creator, does it seem unreasonable that a face-to-face encounter with the One who holds such creative power would not naturally move one to worship Him? It is an expected inner response to God's holiness and majesty that moves the angelic beings to a humble state, and worship naturally flows. An overwhelming sense of awe and joy should come from our recognizing that our Creator's holiness, goodness, and power are far beyond our own limited faculties. Such knowledge should create in us a worshipful heart as well.

Why is this important? For one, it gives us insight into what to expect when we will see God in heaven. A couple of years ago, when I was teaching this subject, I noticed a woman, Joyce Massey, crying as we were discussing the spontaneity of the angels' praise. She was a pillar of faith in my eyes, and I was at a loss as to what brought her to tears. As a teacher, such instances are disturbing, because you are not sure if you inadvertently said something upsetting. She came up to me immediately after class and said, "The lesson was freeing to her." She had always felt that upon going to heaven she "did not have anything to praise God with." For her to compose words of praise to God was a fearful thing. She now understood that upon witnessing God's utter holiness and glory no composing would be necessary. She would not be able to help herself, and praise would naturally flow. While contemplating these thoughts during the lesson, a vision of Switzerland's grandeur popped into her mind, and tears started to flow as she realized God's splendor would be greatly magnified.

Another important reason to develop a proper view of God is that it will be beneficial for our own spiritual well being. A healthy understanding of our relationship with God includes the recognition of who He ultimately is and who we are in relation to Him. The seraphim and four living creatures have a deep appreciation for this. They know their place in regard to God. If our hearts can take on such a humble stance, honoring God will be an innate part of our Christian walk. However, because we live in a society where self-promotion is commonplace, I believe this will be easier said than done.

My guided research at the Harding University Graduate School of Religion laid the foundation for this book. Performing research on God has had a lasting impact on me. I remember one night I was delving into the depths of God's holiness, when suddenly I was struck with the realization of how amazing and wonderful God is. I came face to face with my insignificance in relation to this remarkable, transcendent God I was researching. From the seat at my desk I fell to my knees in tears and honored Him for who He is. My eyes were opened, and heart was laid bare that night. As humility took hold of my being and drove me to my knees, God took on a new exalted position in my life. What an experience! It's a shame it was so long in coming.

Since then I have noted the neglect most churches have in creating an environment that promotes such worshipful responses among its members. Unlike the psalmists of old, today's Christians tend to be more concerned with having an "intimate relationship" with Jesus and "experiencing" God. Not that these things are wrong (in fact they are good), but if they are not kept in balance with the realization that we serve an all-holy and mighty God, we may have a tendency to trivialize Him.

As Christians, our relationship with God is indeed more intimate than our Jewish predecessors. Consider the following: Forgiveness of sins is mediated through Christ, not a priest (Hebrews 9:24-26). God's Spirit indwells us to aid our efforts in becoming like Christ (2 Corinthians 3:18). Jesus states that when two or more are gathered in His name He is among them (Matthew 18:20). God's Spirit also abides among His people in the church today (1 Corinthians 3:16). Family is the context for our Christian life; we are adopted sons of the Father (Romans 8:15), so Jesus in one regard is our brother.

Most certainly, God has created a more intimate relationship with His people today. In fact, it took the extremes of the cross to facilitate this relationship, so it should always be highly esteemed. However, as humans so often do, has our view of God possibly been skewed based on what we want out of the relationship? Perhaps we have conformed God into an image that is not harmonious with who He really is but is more amenable to what we want out of the relationship. As a result, our times of worship and study may gravitate to a focus on self; i.e., desiring knowledge for self-edification, seeking techniques for self-improvement, seeking self-gratifying experiences in worship, and perhaps even looking for opportunities for self-promotion. Our prayers may also be affected. Instead of taking time to honor God, they may just amount to a laundry list of what we want from Him. As a result, we may have unintentionally created a god who serves us versus honoring the One through whose transforming power we are to serve.

With such a perspective, do you think it might have an adverse effect on our worship? If we believe that Jesus and God's Spirit are truly present among us when we are gathered together, is our worship honoring our Lord and God akin to how the angels worship God? Through the prophet Malachi, God warned

Two Old Testament examples serve to warn us that a loss of respect and reverence for God's holiness places us at risk. Moses was not allowed to enter the Promised Land because of his disregard for God; "Because you have not believed Me, to treat Me as holy ... " (Numbers 20:12). Uzzah was killed for touching the ark, which broke a law that was in place to respect God's holy presence; "God struck him down there for his irreverence ... " (2 Samuel 6:7).

Israel that their worship was unacceptable because they failed to give Him the honor and respect He deserves (Malachi 1:6-14). If our view of God is lacking, might the essence of our worship also slip into an unacceptable form?

By becoming out of touch with who God is, our worship services can take on some undesirable features. They most likely will be exhibited by the execution of routines that are empty of meaning, and as a result produce unconscious acts of worship. Are the words we sing truly expressions of the heart and mind that honor God with praise and thanksgiving, or are they meaningless repetition? I remember recently singing the song "Humble Yourself in the Sight of the Lord," when suddenly I realized not much humbling was happening in my heart. Surely I was not alone in my oblivion.

Like the psalmists of old, can we say with conviction and follow through with worshipful hearts on such declarations as these:

> Exalt the LORD our God And worship at His footstool; Holy is He. (Psalm 99:5).

> Great is the LORD, and highly to be praised, And His greatness is unsearchable. ... On the glorious splendor of Your majesty And on Your wonderful works, I will meditate. ... My mouth will speak the praise of the LORD, And all flesh will bless His holy name forever and ever (Psalm 145:3, 5, 21).

> I will sing to the LORD as long as I live; I will sing praise to my God while I have my being. Let my meditation be pleasing to Him; As for me, I shall be glad in the LORD (Psalm 104:33-34).

Along with an intimate relationship with our God as Father, we still need to honor Him as Creator, as sovereign Ruler of the universe, and as a holy God whom no other is like. Rather than just experiencing God, at times we need to *encounter* Him. Taking a lesson from the angels, we should humbly honor and worship our holy Creator.

But what of Jesus; is He just our friend? Have we followed through on our confessions of faith and truly recognized Him as our Lord (Romans 10:9)? Does not Scripture explain that He is King of Kings (Revelation 19:16) and enthroned at the right hand of God (Acts 2:33)? Do we only recognize Him as brother or do we distinguish Him as the head of His church (not our church) (Ephesians 1:22)? We are not the first to struggle with properly honoring Jesus. The author of Hebrews provides a comparison of Jesus and the angels in the first two chapters. Because many Jews around the first century viewed angels as God's created elite, this comparison was probably intended to correct the idea that angels were superior to Jesus and therefore deserved more honor.[24] Paul warns the Colossians not to be led astray by seeking to worship angels (Colossians 2:18). In Revelation, John was scolded by an angel who virtually told him, "Knock it off; worship God not me" (Revelation 19:10). It appears the Hebrew Christians had fallen into the same problem.[25] To set the record straight, the Hebrew writer points out that Jesus is "much better" than the angels because He has inherited the name "Son," correspondingly, the angels are to worship Him (Hebrews 1:4-6). Therefore, the angels should assume their place alongside all creation and worship the exalted Son of God.

> To demonstrate Jesus' divine holiness to His readers, the writer of Hebrews lists the qualities that separate Christ from all creation. Jesus is the heir of all things, agent of creation, glory and image of God, sustainer of all things, purifier of sins, and exalted to the right hand of God (Hebrews 1:2-3).[23]

Back to the Throne Room for Solutions

Let's come back to the throne room and pull together some potential solutions from an experienced group of heavenly worshipers. From the throne room visions so far, we have seen that the angelic approach to worship was one of humility; it was God-centered and selfless. Their declarations called attention to God's magnificent qualities – His holiness, glory, lordship, might, and eternal nature. Their praise radiated conviction, was participatory, and was open for others to hear. Now it's time to turn back to John's throne room vision (Revelation 4), for the worship continues to flow, and there is much for us to learn.

While the four living creatures were praising God, the twenty-four elders that surround the throne were paying close attention. As the living creatures finished their proclamation of praise, the twenty-four elders couldn't help but join in (Revelation 4:8-11). Passionate worship can be contagious. Have you ever observed the heartfelt worship of another? I remember once watching a woman who joyously appeared to be singing directly to God. She was an encouragement to me to dig deeper and engage my heart. Likewise, the four living creatures' worship brought about the twenty-four elders' participation.

> the twenty-four elders will fall down before Him who sits on the throne, and will worship Him who lives forever and ever, and will cast their crowns before the throne, saying, "Worthy are You, our Lord and our God, to receive glory and honor and power; for You created all things, and because of Your will they existed, and were created (vv. 10-11).

At His throne, at the feet of their Lord and God, the twenty-four elders worshiped Him. If we would visualize bringing our praise and prayers before the throne of God in a similar manner, perhaps this would positively set the tone for our worship as well.

Many believe the twenty-four elders are symbolic of God's people. The elders would represent the patriarchs of the twelve tribes and the twelve apostles. This appears unlikely because their song in Revelation 5:9-10 distinguishes them from the redeemed.[26] They more likely represent an angelic order we will discuss at length in Chapter 8 called the Divine Council.

Prostrated hearts are what God deserves. In further humility, the twenty-four elders honored God by casting their crowns before Him. This act of subservience demonstrated their recognition of God's ultimate authority. Perhaps today, many of us wear "artificial" crowns when we encounter God in worship. Whether crowns placed by others or our own self-glorification, we need to recognize their presence. Incidentally, we tend to like our crowns, and they may not want to come off. Nevertheless, to properly worship God, we should humbly remove our crowns and cast them before the Almighty's feet. As the elders continued, God was praised for His creative powers.

As the throne room vision continued in Revelation 5, the living creatures and elders fell down before the Lamb and honored Him in song because of His redemptive work.

> And they sang a new song, saying, "Worthy are You to take the book, and to break its seals; for You were slain, and purchased for God with Your blood men from every tribe and tongue and people and nation. You have made them to be a kingdom and priests to our God; and they will reign upon the earth." (vv. 9-10).

Note how all these beings were basically responding to God and Christ in psalms and songs. This should remind us of some other helpful material. The book of Psalms is an obvious treasure trove. From an angel's point of view, many of these psalms are mankind's cut at declaring God's glory. Their deep, poetic language offers us a rich source of reflective material. Our angelic friends also appear to be pointing us to another source of worshipful material as well.

Alexander Campbell recognized the important effect our hymnals can have on our spirituality. He stated, " ... next to the Bible, no book in the world has such influence on the heart."[27] Our hymnals are full of songs that honor and praise God. Coming from gifted hearts, their lyrics are often steeped in deep meaning, having been inspired by Scripture or moving life experiences. Contemplating many of our songs' stimulating messages should bring a blessing to our devotional times. But I also believe our corporate worship could benefit as well.

An Air Force National Guard chaplain told me of a woman who started preparing herself on Saturday night to enter the worship service the next morning. Now that's noble! Building on this devoted woman's example, technology now offers us a wonderful opportunity. In advance of worship, we could post on our church websites (or send via e-mail) the words to the songs for our upcoming worship service. Can you imagine contemplating and praying over the following before worship?

> Holy, Holy, Holy! All the saints adore Thee,
> Casting down their golden crowns around the crystal sea;
> Cherubim and seraphim falling down before Thee,
> Who wast, and art, and evermore shalt be
>
> Holy, Holy, Holy! Lord God Almighty!
> All Thy works shall praise Thy name, in earth, and sky, and sea:
> Holy, Holy, Holy! merciful and mighty!
> God over all, and blest eternally.[28]

Would not your singing come from a deeper, more expressive place in your soul if we were able to adopt such a practice? Just the simple act of typing these words touched my heart. Driving out meaningless repetition should be the goal in our song services.

Another approach would be to have the song leader share the story behind a song or call attention to meaningful phrases in the song right before singing it. Methods that engender the congregation to respond in song to God and Christ provide a powerful approach to worship. Make it personal; God is present. Deliver your offering of song directly to Him. Whatever technique your congregation or you personally want to use, our God deserves hearts that genuinely honor Him.

The worship recorded in Revelation 5 continues to be contagious. Some of the angels must have said, "No way are we missing out on this good stuff!" So an innumerable amount of angels jump in with the elders and living creatures to thunderously proclaim the next psalm of praise.

> Worthy is the Lamb that was slain to receive power and riches and wisdom and might and honor and glory and blessing (v. 12).

What a scene! You are probably saying, "Hey, I want in on the next psalm of praise!" I think you will get your chance when all creation joins this happy angel chorus.

> And every created thing which is in heaven and on the earth and under the earth and on the sea, and all things in them, I heard saying, "To Him who sits on the throne, and to the Lamb, be blessing and honor and glory and dominion forever and ever" (v. 13).

And the scene closed with the living creatures giving their hearty approval by saying "Amen, Amen, Amen!" The elders again could not help themselves; they fell at the feet of their Creator and the Savior and worshiped (Revelation 5:14). Now that's a "worship" service! If I was an angel, I think I would be high-fiving my angelic buddies. Absolutely awesome!

The angels' worship gives us hope. They provide us with a picture of how devoted hearts worship. They invite us to encounter God and Christ in a way we might have overlooked. In all humility, their worship attests to God and Christ's glorious attributes and what they have accomplished. To them, God and the Lamb are worthy. Worship is the only possible outcome. How about you?

Let's not allow our worship to stop when we leave our church buildings. Our personal devotional time should periodically include a dose of encountering God. Without it, our journey to be conformed into the image of Christ will likely be corrupted. God can be encountered, not only in the praise and thanksgiving psalms, but throughout much of His Word. Many stories provide excellent segue ways for our personal worship of God and Jesus, such as the Creation story, the Exodus from Egypt, the throne room visions (Isaiah 6:1-6; Daniel 7; Revelation 4-5), the nativity and crucifixion stories – and I am sure you have your favorites. The first chapter in many of the epistles often contains worshipful thoughts as well. Make sure you set this time aside as worship. This is not a time to evaluate your spirituality or satisfy intellectual pursuits. Be intentional; worship your Lord and God. Let prayers, songs, poetry, or praise go before their thrones. They are worthy.

Questions

1. Have there been times in your life when you believe that you have encountered our holy God and His majesty? Take a few minutes to think this through. What prompted such a realization? What were some of your responses?

2. In creating the narration of Isaiah 6:1-6, how did Isaiah use the seraphim as a means to draw his readers to the holiness of God?

3. Due to the supernatural character of the seraphim, we may be able to understand how some might be misled to worship such beings. What should our view be as to the "position" of the angelic beings?

4. How might we conform God into an image that is not consistent with who He is? What are the implications of these actions?

5. In this chapter, we reviewed several instances of angelic beings worshiping God. How did they approach God in worship? What methods did they use? What are some specific things that they honor and praise God (or Christ) for? How should we apply this information to our own corporate and personal times of worship?

6. Are you pleased with your own offerings of praise and worship to God? How might your local congregation create a worship experience that allows us to respond in ways that honor
   God's holiness, yet remain true to God's commands for proper
   worship?

7. Has observing others during times of worship inspired your
   own worship to be better? Are there any concerns with this
   that we should keep in mind?

8. If you incorporate time to honor God during your personal de-
   votions, what impact could that have on your spirituality? If left
   out, how might this impact your spiritual formation?

Chapter 4

Holy and Fallen Angels

I was looking in the visions in my mind
as I lay on my bed, and behold, an angelic watcher,
a holy one, descended from heaven (Daniel 4:13).

At one point in my life, softball was one of my favorite pastimes. The church that I attended was involved in a national softball organization made up of local church league teams from around the U.S. Our team happened to be fairly competitive for several years. The team's most successful year came about when we finished fifth in a tournament that included the best church teams from the Southeast region of the U.S. This level of play was filled with excitement and great fun. I must admit that ministry took a back seat to our team's relentless focus on winning. Even so, several meaningful relationships developed and some seeds were planted due to the Christian environment we aspired to maintain. Eventually, we had several of our more gifted athletes move out of the area, so we lost our ability to compete at a high level. Our strategy shifted from being a competitive team to becoming a recreational team that focused on fellowship. This was a hard adjustment for me, because I loved the elevated level of play; but God had a lesson for me to learn.

As the next season approached, a new family moved in the area and started attending our congregation. It did not take me long to approach the man of this family about playing on our softball team. After all, this guy was a pretty good-sized fellow and looked like he had the capability to do some damage to a softball. He was really excited about the opportunity, and once the games started no one took more joy from the experience than our new teammate. Clearly he enjoyed the light-hearted competition, but I think more than anything else he simply cherished the camaraderie of his teammates. Unapparent to me, something much deeper was transpiring within the heart of this lovable man. Out of the blue, he decided to give his life to Christ. Not only did we have a new teammate; we now had a new brother.

My closest friend on the team later informed me that our new brother's participation on the softball team actually played a key role in his conversion. From my experience with our competitive teams, I had come to believe that church softball was not a good evangelistic tool. So I was anxious to hear his explanation. Our new convert's impression of the men at our church initially came from attending the worship service. To him, they all appeared "so holy," and a feeling of inadequacy took hold of him. He believed that he could never live up to such standards. Once he spent some time with us on the softball field, he started to see our humanity creep out a little. By now, you might suspect we were all a bunch of heathens once we escaped the four walls of the church building, but this was not really the case. Throughout the league our team was known for conducting itself in a godly manner, but by being in such close quarters with us, our new brother would occasionally see a few human flaws sneak out. Nevertheless, at the same time he could observe our commitment to honoring God in our behavior. As a result, our softball team brought him to the realization that absolute holiness belongs only to God; mankind may aspire to that holiness, but we all rely on Christ's blood to make us truly holy.

Through this experience, I learned that a church softball team could serve as a powerful ministerial tool, but I would like to draw your attention to something else. Ethical (or moral) holiness can be intimidating to others. In the previous chapter, we saw that God's transcendent holiness produces an awe or godly fear within us. In a

> The Seraphim's proclamation of God's holiness (Isaiah 6:3) served to glorify Him but also may have functioned as a warning to Isaiah that he must be cleansed prior to standing in God's presence.[29]

comparable manner, God's absolute moral holiness humbles us, because it causes our many imperfections to come to light. Similarly, when we come in contact with others who live holy lives, we may become intimidated by their excellent behavior, like our softball friend.

When Isaiah stood in the presence of God in the throne room vision (Isaiah 6), not only did the awe of the Almighty's glory and majesty overtake him, but he also became immediately aware of his own moral inadequacies. Check out his concerns; "Woe is me, for I am ruined! Because I am a man of unclean lips, And I live among a people of unclean lips; For my eyes have seen the King, the LORD of hosts" (Isaiah 6:5). Isaiah's moral flaws were further highlighted by the subsequent action of one of the seraphim. Before God commissioned Isaiah to be a prophet, one of the seraphim took a coal from the altar and touched Isaiah's lips with it to take away his sins (vv. 6-7). After being cleansed, Isaiah stood before God, ready for dialogue and now useful for service.

Understanding God's attribute of moral holiness should be of considerable importance to us because moral imperfection is what relationally separates us from Him. An intriguing story concerning the angels will help shed some light on this characteristic of God, as well as how these heavenly creatures are referenced in God's Word. Also, with holiness being intimidating to others, what implications does this bring to light concerning ministry?

Fallen Angels

We humans are considered volitional creatures or beings of choice. Many situations come our way every day that we must evaluate with our moral compass to determine a course of action. Because God blessed us with free moral choice, He consequently does not force His will upon us. If I want to lie or tell the truth, that is my choice. If I go against my society's norms and get caught, I will have to bear the consequences of my action. If I go against God's laws, I risk separation from Him. God's holy nature cannot tolerate communion with our unholy attitudes and actions. Of course, Christ's blood can bring about forgiveness if we repent of our unholy choices and seek to live righteously.

But what of angels; are they volitional beings? The psalmist states, "Bless the LORD, you His angels, Mighty in strength, who perform His word, Obeying the voice of His word!" (Psalm 103:20). This verse appears to support the idea that angels are beings of choice. Upon hearing God's voice, they process His words and choose to obey. Jude and Peter also support the idea that angels are volitional by referencing the following tragic angelic event:

> And angels who did not keep their own domain, but abandoned their proper abode, He has kept in eternal bonds under darkness for the judgment of the great day, Just as Sodom and Gomorrah and the cities around them, since they in the same way as these indulged in gross immorality and went after strange flesh, are exhibited as an example in undergoing the punishment of eternal fire (Jude 1:6-7).

> For if God did not spare angels when they sinned, but cast them into hell and committed them to pits of darkness, reserved for judgment (2 Peter 2:4).

Both of these verses presuppose the angels made a decision. There was a "domain" to keep, but they chose against it. Sinning infers that the angels broke some divine ordinance they were to live by. I submit that not only are angels volitional, but their choices have eternal ramifications.

I want to share with you the significance of the angels' behavior as it relates to God; but you are probably wondering, what in heaven's name did these angels do? So before I continue, I need to share with you what incident Jude and Peter made reference to in these passages.

In Genesis 6, a strange little story appears prior to the flood narrative and may be the reason for its necessity.

> Now it came about, when men began to multiply on the face of the land, and daughters were born to them, that the sons of God saw that the daughters of men were beautiful; and they took wives for themselves, whomever they chose. Then the LORD said, "My Spirit shall not strive with man forever, because he also is flesh; nevertheless his days shall be one hundred and twenty years." The Nephilim were on the earth in those days, and also afterward, when the sons of God came in to the daughters of men, and they bore children to them. Those were the mighty men who were of old, men of renown (vv. 1-4).

To understand this story, we need to figure out who are the "daughters of men" and "sons of God." One popular theory proposes that the daughters of men were from the lineage of Cain, while the sons of God were from the lineage of Seth.[30] This was my preferred theory for years, but how would such a union produce Nephilim (giants or extremely violent men)?

Another popular theory of the Genesis 6:1-4 story involves the sexual union of angels (sons of God) to beautiful women on the earth. Previously I discounted this theory because it sounded too much like a fable. Perhaps in a fantasy such as *Lord of the Rings* I would expect such a tale, but not in God's Word. However, after continued research on this subject, I now consider this my preferred theory. Because of this theory's extraordinary nature, I would like to share with you a summary of my rationale for accepting it. First, the author of Job used the phrase "sons of God" to refer to angels several times (Job 1:6; 2:1; 38:7), therefore such a use by the author of Genesis would be consistent with other biblical usage.

A second crucial point requires us to answer two questions. What actually did the first century A.D. Judeo-Christian world believe in regard to the Genesis 6:1-4 story? And how does that relate to Jude and Peter's comments concerning the judgment of the angels in the above passages? By the first century A.D., Jewish tradition of Genesis 6:1-4 attested to the common belief that angels had defiled themselves by having sexual relations with women producing giant offspring. Jewish literature and historical writings abounded with references to this belief. *First Enoch* provides the most detailed account, but many other documents mention this story to varying levels of detail, such as *2 Baruch, Jubilees, Testament of Reuben, Testament of Naphtali, The Damascus Document*, Philo's *On the Giants*, Josephus' *Antiquities*, and two Dead Sea Scroll Documents – *Genesis Apocryphon* and *The Book of Giants*.[31] The author of *1 Enoch* states the following concerning God's judgment of the angels:

> ... For what reason have you abandoned the high, holy, and eternal heaven; and slept with women and defiled yourselves with the daughters of the people, taking wives, acting like the children of the earth, and begetting giant sons? Surely you, you [used to be] holy, spiritual, the living ones, [possessing] eternal life; but (now) you have defiled yourselves with women, and with the blood of the flesh begotten children, you have lusted with the blood of the people, like them producing blood and flesh, (which) die and perish. On that account, I have given you wives in order that (seeds) might be sown upon them and children born by them, so that the deeds that are done upon the earth will not be withheld from you. Indeed you, formerly you were spiritual, (having) eternal life, and immortal in all the generations of the world. That is why (formerly) I did not make wives for you, for the dwelling of the spiritual beings of heaven is heaven (1 Enoch 15:3-7).[32]

From now on you will not be able to ascend into heaven unto all eternity, but you shall remain inside the earth, imprisoned all the days of eternity (1 Enoch 14:5-6).[33]

The following are some samples from several of the other documents that promote this commonly-held traditional belief.

And when the children of men began to multiply on the surface of the earth and daughters were born to them, that the angels of the Lord saw in a certain year of that jubilee that they were good to look at. And they took wives for themselves from all of those whom they chose. And they bore children for them; and they were the giants. And injustice increased upon the earth, and all flesh corrupted its way... (Jubilees 5:1-2).[34]

For it was thus that they charmed the Watchers, who were before the Flood. As they continued looking at the women, they were filled with desire for them and perpetrated the act in their minds. Then they were transformed into human males, and while the women were cohabiting with their husbands they appeared to them. Since the women's minds were filled with lust for these apparitions, they gave birth to giants. For the Watchers were disclosed to them as being as high as the heavens
(Testament of Reuben 5:6).[35]

And some of them came down and mingled themselves with women. At that time they who acted like this were tormented in chains (2 Baruch 56:12-13) (early 2nd century A.D.).[36]

For many angels of God accompanied with women, and begat sons that proved unjust, and despisers of all that was good, on account of the confidence they had in their own strength; for the tradition is that these men did what resembled the acts of those whom the Grecians called giants (Josephus, *Antiquities* 1.3.1).[37]

The evidence appears virtually indisputable as to what the widespread view of the Genesis 6:1-4 story would have been when Peter and Jude wrote their epistles. For this reason, they did not need to elaborate on why the angels fell because their audience was already acquainted with the story. If someone today mentions "9-11," we do not need them to expound on the actual event. Its

> Justin Martyr (A.D. 100-165), one of the earliest Christian writers, made this comment concerning the angels' fall; "But the angels transgressed this appointment, and were captivated by love of women, and begat children" (Justin Martyr, 1 Apology 5).

various aspects readily come to mind. Likewise, because of the angelic fall story's familiarity in the first century A.D., Peter and Jude's audience required only a brief mention of this event to bring to mind the greater details.

I am not suggesting any of the above documents are inspired nor am I suggesting Peter and Jude would have viewed them that way. Nonetheless, these documents are valuable for shedding light on some of the commonly-held beliefs of the day. Jude most certainly was familiar with *1 Enoch* because he later quotes it in Jude 1:14-15, so it is reasonable to assume that he would also have been aware of the fall of the angels story within it. Peter and Jude's succinct approach in mentioning this story may also indicate that they did not agree with everything in these documents. There does appear to be much authorial embellishment concerning this story. Perhaps the story's basic premise was true, but a fable was built around it. Sounds a little like Hollywood.

This brings me to my last point. Jude states in verse 7 that Sodom and Gomorrah's sin resembled the angels' because they both "indulged in gross immorality and went after strange flesh."

This statement strongly implies that Jude believed the commonly-held account that the angels had sinned in a sexual way. I once thought the concept of angels having sexual relations with human women was ridiculous. Why would spiritual beings lust after women and desire to have sexual relations with them? Did not Jesus infer that angels had no reason to procreate (Matthew 22:30)? But as I mentioned before, angels at times have come in the form of mankind (e.g. see Genesis 19 and Hebrews 13:2). If they truly take on the attributes of a man, would not the potential to lust after women lie crouching at the door?[38] I know of no other temptation more compelling to men than sexual lust. If the angels came to earth as men during Noah's time and were impressed by the physical beauty of women, their heads may have been spinning with the power of sexual arousal.

Sometimes we want to know more than God has chosen to reveal to us. In all humility, I recognize the amount of inspired Scripture on this topic is limited and vague, and my own conclusions fall in the realm of opinion. Yet I hope I have been able to remove your blinders to consider new possibilities. Every time I walk into the theological library at the Harding Graduate School of Religion, I am truly humbled, because I have only nipped at the heels of the knowledge that lies before me. New insights that challenge our understanding provide us with opportunities to enrich our faith. If we will prayerfully and thoughtfully seek God's truth in evaluating them, not only will our knowledge increase, but my experience has been, that we will also be drawn closer to our God and Savior. Understanding Peter and Jude's reference to the fall of the angels has been an interesting aside, but more serious implications to these passages still await us.

Peter and Jude highlight a difference between God's treatment of the angels and us. When the angels sinned by not staying within the domain God had assigned them, He temporarily passed judgment upon them. He has bound them until the final judgment at Christ's return, when they will be permanently sentenced. Pretty serious stuff!

When I was in fourth grade, I became pretty good at making all kinds of fun creations out of notebook paper. I sat in the back of the classroom, where I could construct my contraptions without being noticed. One day, with the sink right behind me and a packet of Kool-Aid in my pocket, the temptation to make a paper cup overtook me. I am sure you can imagine what happened next. By the time I took the first sip of my cleverly prepared beverage, this silly girl started giggling. For disturbing the class, I was ushered off to the principal's office. I can still remember being more nervous than a long-tailed cat in a room full of rocking chairs, as I waited outside the principal's office. I knew some cruel and unusual punishment awaited me; but when all was said and done, I was allowed to come back to class. I had been punished but given a second chance; the angels did not receive a second chance.

There are those in our society who become incarcerated for their criminal actions. Only for extreme offenses do they stay in prison for life; yet even those inmates can still receive forgiveness from God for their sins. In some cases, we may struggle to accept that forgiveness is truly within their grasp. I still vividly recall watching the evening news and listening to the reporter tell of the heinous crimes committed by Jeffrey Dahmer. In my eyes, Dahmer's crimes of murder, dismemberment, and cannibalism make him the most evil person that I can remember in my generation. Yet some loving soul took the time to teach the gospel to this twisted man, and he was baptized for the forgiveness of his sins. Assuming Dahmer had truly repented, as the preacher who baptized him believed, such forgiveness speaks to the enormity of God's grace in Christ Jesus.[39] When we sing there is "power in the blood," wow, is there ever! Unlike Dahmer, forgiveness does not appear to be on the horizon for angels who sin.

Why do the angels not receive a second chance? Does not Christ's blood cover them along with humankind? The writer of Hebrews provides a helpful statement:

For assuredly He does not give help to angels, but He gives help to the descendant of Abraham. Therefore, He had to be made like His brethren in all things, that He might become a merciful and faithful high priest in things pertaining to God, to make propitiation for the sins of the people (2:16-17).

Jesus' redeeming sacrifice was for Abraham's descendants; "for the sins of the *people.*" Paul expounded in Galatians 3 that faith in Jesus Christ makes us Abraham's offspring, and the eternal life that results from such faith was offered to the world (John 3:16). God's redemptive work through Christ targeted humankind, not angels. Unlike humans who have access to Jesus' sanctifying blood, angels have no hope of regaining their holiness.

I feel badly for our heavenly co-servants, but an important truth about God has been revealed to us in the judgment of these fallen angels – God's perfect holiness is in total opposition to sin and cannot permanently co-exist with it. Unlike us humans, these angels had witnessed firsthand God's holiness and majesty. To experience and partake of God's holiness in the heavenly realm provided the angels with an understanding of God and His ways that is currently beyond our comprehension. Because they pursued a path of rebellion against God's holy nature, they placed themselves in an unrecoverable state. Because of their unholiness, God removed them from His presence and bound them until Judgment Day. From their horrible mistake, the angels have taught us that holiness is an absolute requirement if we are to have a relationship with God.

Holy Angels

Fortunately, it appears that most angels have chosen to be holy. We can infer from Scripture that myriads and myriads of angels continue to loyally serve God and keep their holy calling (Daniel 7:10; Hebrews 12:22; Revelation 5:11). If *1 Enoch* has any semblance of reliability in its "fall of the angels" story, the author reports that only two hundred angels fell (*1 Enoch* 6:6). Compared to the vast number of angels that exist, perhaps we can deduce that only a small percentage fell. Whatever the case, heaven's halls still appear to be filled with an immense quantity of God's holy angels.

How do we actually know the angels are holy? Predominantly because that is the way God's Word often refers to them. Jesus designated His heavenly followers as holy; "the Son of Man will also be ashamed of him when He comes in the glory of His Father with the holy angels" (Mark 8:38). Daniel also attested to their holy status; "Then I heard a holy one speaking, and another holy one said to that particular one ... " (Daniel 8:13). Angels even spoke of one another with holy regard. In Revelation, an angel announced that those who worship the beast will be punished "in the presence of the holy angels" (Revelation 14:10). Luke used the title "an angel of God" for the heavenly host who liberated Peter from prison (Acts 12:7). These designations carry with them the idea of the angel's fellowship with their holy Creator. They are holy in likeness to God's holiness. That is why Luke can use the title "an angel of God," because to be "of God" one must be holy and consequently may represent Him as His agent in ministry.

While at NASA, I learned the criticality of making sure everyone involved in our technical projects understood and marched to the same mission goals. NASA's safety mission stood at the heart of all our programs, and its creed of "Safety First" was deeply ingrained into the heart and soul of our work culture. Adhering to sound safety principles and practices directly related to the success of our human space flight endeavors. For example, if a work team was replacing a component within the Space Shuttle's liquid oxygen system and failed to take the proper precautions to prevent contaminants from entering the system, they may inadvertently introduce an explosive hazard. This lack of attention to common safety practices could put the lives of the astronauts at stake, as well as risking catastrophic damage to a multi-billion dollar government asset.

God has a holiness mission. Those who desire to be in communion with Him must conform to a holiness consistent with His nature; we are to be holy because God is holy (1 Peter 1:15-16). God's kingdom has been established to aid in the success of this mission for each individual. Jesus became incarnate and suffered the cross to assure mankind has the ability to achieve the desired state of holiness. The Holy Spirit's sanctifying work is to transform the Christian into leading a life of holiness. God's Word equips us with the principles of holiness, along with practical examples, both good and bad. Upon our conversion, God places us within the church where we join others and receive support from those on the same holiness journey we are undertaking. God especially equips leaders, preachers, various ministers, and teachers to help us succeed. God desires mission success for us, and we all need to be on the same page with Him to succeed. Eternity is at stake – angels can attest to that.

We live in a world hostile to our holy calling. Daily lured to pursue money, pleasure, power, notoriety and the like, our souls are constantly assailed with enticements to stray from a life of holiness. The world's promises of happiness place us on shaky ground, but the writer of Hebrews reminds us that God's kingdom is unshakable. God not only unites the Christian with Himself, Christ, and the church, but to a heavenly realm that includes myriads of angels that all comprise an immovable kingdom, a holy kingdom (Hebrews 12:18-29).

But what are we to make of this new fellowship with the holy angels? The writer of Hebrews again points out that on occasion we may even be touched by their holiness; angels are "ministering spirits, sent out to render service for the sake of those who will inherit salvation" (Hebrews 1:14). Although, we may not recognize their presence; "Do not neglect to show hospitality to strangers, for by this some have entertained angels without knowing it" (13:2). Perhaps as this hostile world oppresses us and tries to lead us away from God's holy ways, He sends angels on missions of mercy to open our eyes to pathways of holiness. What better way can angels minister to those who are to "inherit salvation" than to facilitate this very thing?

Angelic Behavior

If we should aspire to any angelic quality presented to us in God's Word, the most important would be their holiness. To clarify what personal holiness consists of, let's examine one of Peter's teachings on the subject. Peter let his first century readers know that holiness is not some abstract religious construct.

> As obedient children, do not be conformed to the former lusts which were yours in your ignorance, but like the Holy One who called you, be holy yourselves also in all your behavior; because it is written, "You shall be holy, for I am holy" (1 Peter 1:14-16).

Peter was not referring to how they conducted worship, but how they lived out their lives in the world around them. Holiness pertains to "all" our behavior; behavior that separates us and demonstrates our difference from the ways of the world. Our God and Father has a holy character; and as His children, we are to conform to this same character.

God's character has been magnificently revealed to us in Christ Jesus. Paul's concept that Christians should be "conformed to the image of His Son" (Romans 8:29), is another way of expressing our need to become holy. As we take on the character traits of Christ, the subsequent behavior produced from this new internal orientation should be holy. The Spirit has an active role in this ongoing process; "But we all, with unveiled face, beholding as in a mirror the glory of the Lord, are being transformed into the same image from glory to glory, just as from the Lord, the Spirit" (2 Corinthians 3:18). Becoming like Christ allows us to have fellowship with God because it produces a holiness within us that is consistent with His.

The Greek terms for sanctify and saint are derived from the word for holy (*hagios*). Once we are made holy (sanctify), we become holy ones (saints).

It is true that Christ's blood sanctifies us (makes us holy), but God's Word also describes the ongoing process of sanctification (or process of becoming holy), which is directly connected to eternal life (Romans 6:22; 2 Thessalonians 2:13; Hebrews 12:14). I have found the comparison of "becoming a Marine" helpful in understanding this. When you take the oath to become a Marine, you are officially a Marine, yet you must still "become" a Marine. Once you make it through basic training and are tested on the battlefield, you truly "become" a Marine. As Christ's blood cleanses us (and continues to cleanse us), we become one of God's holy ones. Yet we have a lifelong journey ahead of us "to become holy"; i.e., to change who we are deep inside and take on the character traits of Christ. We are honed on the battlefield of the world, where our forming holy character fights against a bombardment of temptations. Allied with the Holy Spirit, hopefully our resultant behaviors become steadily more consistent with our holy calling as a child of God.

What of our earlier observation that people who exhibit holy behavior may unintentionally be intimidating to others? Does this stand in the way of our reaching out to others? The answer is both yes and no. No, because without good role models to show others what a life of holiness looks like, we have a bigger problem. Paul encourages the Philippians to follow his example, and those "who walk according to the pattern you have in us" (Philippians 3:17). New Christians need good role models to show them the ropes, like an apprentice learns from the highly skilled master craftsmen. I am not suggesting that we can change our character strictly through practice, but we must start somewhere. After our conversion, a great deal of transformative work needs to be done on our hearts. Some facets of our character have been very problematic to change. Seeing a role model's holy conduct in diverse situations will help us understand what we should aspire to, hone in on where we need to change, and reinforce our desire to change through seeing godly results. Having a Christian role model provides us with another important spiritual tool, along with Bible study and prayer, to facilitate building a mature faith. A strong faith accompanied by the Spirit's sanctifying work is a recipe for success in developing holy character (2 Thessalonians 2:13). Obviously, our character traits will never be like Christ's in all ways, at least this side of eternity, but our goal should be to progress to the point where we can serve as role models for others.

And yes, our holy conduct can inadvertently stand in the way of reaching out to others. When a person's inadequacies are inadvertently brought to light because of our holy lifestyle, it can be hurtful. If you are like me, you don't want to experience pain. We would rather stay in a comfortable place, even if it means living with character flaws that produce unwanted behaviors. How do we then mitigate the intimidating tendency holiness has on others? This is where activities like softball can be a powerful ministry, even if it is not intentional. We need to replace their discomfort in tension with comfort. Rather than being in the "sanctity" of the church building, we come together in the neutral environment of a softball field. On this field of clay and turf, we share a common knowledge of the game, and the same spirited goals. Don't worry, though, competition has a way of bringing about opportunities for us to exhibit godly behavior that may just cause others to notice and say to themselves, "hmmm." In a competitive environment, all kinds of situations arise – we may be unfairly called out by an umpire, a member of another team may taunt us, or someone on either team may become injured while sliding into a base. Such circumstances offer opportunities for holy responses. Not demeaning the umpire, defusing another's taunting, and praying and caring for the injured will show our good character, which in all likelihood will be very different from what those vigilant eyes and ears of others have experienced in the world.

There have only been a few individuals in my life whose godly lifestyles exuded an aura of holiness that initially made me uncomfortable to be in their presence. One such man was an elder in a church I attended several years ago. Even though his nature appeared impeccable, he made a point of being approachable. He took great interest in me and had my wife and me over for dinner several times. It is amazing how mealtime conversations open new horizons in relationships. Some of the most strategic times I spent with co-workers at NASA occurred during the relaxing setting of lunchtime conversations. This noble elder also eased my discomfort by sharing his hobbies with me. By revealing his interests and showing me his various projects, his humanness began to ring out. I still held his admirable conduct in high regard, but I began to relate to him as a person. This opened a door for me to view him as a role model. Over the years he learned my gifts and skills and often encouraged me to serve the Lord in various capacities. If he had not challenged me to teach a middle school class on Wednesday nights about twenty years ago, some of my gifts might still lay dormant and writing a book like this may never have come to pass. Much power lies in the art of being hospitable and genuine with others. Accompanied by patience, these gracious qualities should be able to help our outreach endeavors.

Holiness is not an option; our eternal ambitions depend on it. But God also desires His children to be holy for an additional reason. God's angels who became unholy were no longer useful to serve Him. God needs servants in this world to reach out to the lost who desperately need holiness in their lives. To be useful to God in ministry (service) we must be holy. Paul told Timothy that it is the sanctified believer who is useful to God for good works (2 Timothy 2:21). Peter also disclosed that as a "holy nation" we are fit to "proclaim the excellencies" of the God who called us (1 Peter 2:9). If I am teaching someone about Christ, and they see me steal a stapler from work, do you think I will be able to make any headway with them? Probably not! God does not expect perfection, Christ's blood takes care of that; but for us to be "effective" workers in His kingdom, a holy lifestyle is a necessity.

Parenthood brought many wonderful experiences to my life. However, some parental experiences can be labeled as less than wonderful. One such incident occurred when we took our daughter to Disney World when she was fairly young. I cannot remember too much about that day, except one ride that would scar my memory forever. After reading the brochure, "It's a Small World" appeared to be the perfect ride to take my young daughter on. How could I go wrong by selecting a ride where she could enjoy animated dolls from around the world? After embarking upon a little boat, we were slowly taken down a fairy tale river where dolls from around the world greeted us around every bend with a chorus of the song "It's a Small World." As luck would have it, the ride broke down about half way through, but the dolls kept right on singing their joyous tune. After about twenty minutes, the ride started again, and we entered a new country where the dolls sang their theme song in a foreign language. Guess what happened next? You got it; the ride broke down again, and then again. Over and over I had to endure this song. What once was a merry little tune turned into a hideous, loathsome caterwaul. It was *Twilight Zone* at the Disney park; pure torture.

On a much more serious note, do you think we unconsciously torment God through our unholy actions? I often ponder this question. Over and over throughout life our weaknesses raise their ugly heads, and we succumb to temptation and sin. Because God dwells in His people through the Holy Spirit (1 Corinthians 6:19; Ephesians 3:16; Romans 5:5), I am sure our sin deeply grieves Him; possibly in ways we do not understand. Paul told the Corinthians that because God dwelled in them, they must turn away from everything that was not compatible with His holiness.

> Do not be bound together with unbelievers; for what partnership have righteousness and lawlessness, or what fellowship has light with darkness? ... For we are the temple of the

living God; just as God said, "I will dwell in them and walk among them; And I will be their God, and they shall be my people. Therefore, come out from their midst and be separate," says the Lord. "And do not touch what is unclean; and I will welcome you. And I will be a father to you, And you shall be sons and daughters to Me," Says the Lord Almighty. Therefore, having these promises, beloved, let us cleanse ourselves from all defilement of flesh and spirit, perfecting holiness in the fear of God (2 Corinthians 6:14, 16-18; 7:1).

If Christ's blood did not continue to cleanse us as we "walk in the Light" (or pursue holiness) (1 John 1:7), I am sure our holy God would have nothing to do with us. I am so thankful for God's sanctifying presence within me. I want the Spirit's rivers of living water to forever flow from my innermost being (John 7:38-39). Life as a Christian would be hopeless without Him. Let us be committed to leading holy lives so that honor and glory will be brought upon our beloved God who has chosen to take up residence inside our hearts. Amen!

Questions

1. Have you ever felt uncomfortable in the presence of someone whom you considered particularly holy? Why did you feel that way? Did you later feel at ease with this individual? If so, what helped you overcome your discomfort?

2. When developing ministries, what techniques should we consider to introduce others to holiness? How about on an individual level?

3. Why do you think Jude and Peter did not expound further on the fall of the angels story they referenced? How might that be relevant to our understanding these verses?

4. What do Jude and Peter's comments on the fall of the angels teach us about God? What significance does this have for us?

5. Why do you think the angels were not somehow offered forgiveness when they sinned?

6. Why does God want us to be holy? How has He equipped the Christian to attain holiness? Do angels have a role in this activity? If so, how?

7. What is meant by ethical or moral holiness (ref. 1 Peter 1:14-16)? How has God's holy character been revealed to us? How does conforming to the image of Christ relate to holiness?

8. Holiness has eternal ramifications, but what are some other reasons for us to be holy?

Part 3

Love of God

Love Prelude

Do you remember your favorite stuffed animal when you were a child? I would dare to guess it was much loved and quite cuddly. For inanimate objects, stuffed animals have a mysterious way of bringing comfort into our lives. When my daughter was about ten years old, she had to go through a pretty complicated surgery. Because her mom worked in the medical field, my daughter had at least one parent who was familiar with hospital procedures. On the day of the surgery, I had a great deal of nervous energy and believed that I should do something to reassure my daughter. Suddenly a bright idea hit me, and I was off to find the hospital gift shop to buy her a teddy bear. I found one that passed my requirements – cute and cuddly. When I gave her the teddy bear, she immediately wrapped her arms around it. That was the birth of Randy Bear. Randy has received a ridiculous amount of cuddling in his life, and even as a young adult my daughter still gives Randy his fair share of love.

As God's attributes go, love is the "cuddly" one. It is the part of His character that gives us the most comfort. For example, God's holiness can be intimidating and His justice unsettling, but God's love is warm and inviting. Expressions of love that come our way in life are usually treasured. Once we truly comprehend what God accomplished for us in Christ Jesus, such a love becomes forever cherished. We will want to wrap our arms around it and never let it go. Great security is found in the loving arms of God. In actuality, we are dependent on His love, and fortunately He richly bestows it.

When we say that "God is love," what are we specifically saying about Him? God's love is a multi-dimensional trait in Scripture and includes benevolence, grace, mercy (compassion), and long-suffering.[40] These different aspects of love are interrelated and typically work harmoniously together. God's benevolent love is conveyed in the New Testament term *agape*. This is an others-seeking, sacrificial love; a love that puts others' interests before one's own.

A number of years ago I was having lunch with one of my sisters and her husband at a quaint little family-run eatery. During the meal, the waitress accidentally knocked over a full glass of milk into my brother-in-law's lap. Remorse immediately overcame this poor waitress, as she hurriedly tried to clean up the mess. I can still remember how visibly shaken this kind young woman became. My sister and brother-in-law kept cool heads throughout this unfortunate incident, but what happened next left a lasting impression on me. Expecting them to leave a small tip, my sister surprised me by leaving a fifty percent tip. She looked at me and said, "The waitress is having a rough day and hopefully the tip will brighten things up for her." That's *agape*.

As God looked upon His creation, He saw humankind in a miserable state, marred by sin and separated from Him. Even though humanity was responsible for creating the chasm that separated themselves from their holy God, they stood helpless to repair the rift. To re-establish a relationship with His beloved creation, God brought about the ultimate demonstration of benevolent love. The Bible's most famous phrase succinctly captures the extent and purpose of God's love; "For God so loved the world, that He gave His only begotten Son, that whoever believes in Him should not perish, but have eternal life" (John 3:16). God loves us so much that He took on the cross that we could have life. That's "amazing" *agape*.

God undoubtedly desires the best for us and seeks after our welfare, but did He expect anything from humanity prior to reaching out benevolently to us?[41] For example, if you sacrificially work long hours to support your children while they attend college, do you expect anything from them before you graciously pay their tuition and room and board? I would hope you expect them to show a commitment to studying versus partying. Yet God's love was extended and continues to be extended without any prior expectations on mankind's part. In truth, God considered us enemies because of sin but despite our failings He chose to demonstrate His love for us through Christ's sacrificial death (Romans 5:8-10). This is grace – remarkable grace. By adding the dimension of grace to God's love, He extends love as an undeserved act of kindness. As in the case of the accident-laden waitress, she did not "deserve" a generous tip. It was benevolently given to her as a gift.

Biblical grace is obviously much more than a prayer before a meal. As the centerpiece of God's offer of salvation, grace stood in radical opposition to the Jews' legalistic traditions. To the Jews, only strict adherence to the Law made an individual "worthy" of being considered one of God's own. Our own culture also stands counter to the concept of grace; each of us must "earn" our way through life. We earn grades, wages, respect, and trust, but we had better become used to the notion of grace. Because when it comes to the forgiveness of sins, we can do nothing to earn this cherished standing. The cost is too high. God had to pay the price for us. God, the Son, "earned" our redemption upon the cruel cross of Calvary. We can only accept it as a gift; and what a wonderful gift it is.

Paul eloquently explained this concept to the Ephesians; "For by grace you have been saved through faith; and that not of yourselves, it is the gift of God; not as a result of works, that no one may boast" (Ephesians 2:8-9). Paul's words to the Roman church serve to convict us that "all have sinned and fall short of the glory of God," but also provide hope that forgiveness can be received "as a gift by His grace through the redemption which is in Christ Jesus" (Romans 3:24). Forgiven and liberated from the death grip of sin, we can now pursue the One who loves us. God's grace is nothing short of perplexing. If you are like me, you probably have asked the question, "Why does God care so much about me?" Hopefully, the next dimension of His love will shed some light on the answer.

God's mercy is the quality that lies behind His acts of benevolence and grace. As God sees His beloved creation in a broken and pitiful condition because of sin's effect on the human soul,

His compassionate nature compels Him to heal our spiritual ills.[42] God's grace and benevolence thus reaches out from God's merciful nature. Paul expresses this idea while reflecting upon the former worldly nature of the Ephesians:

> But God, being rich in mercy, because of His great love with which He loved us, even when we were dead in our transgressions, made us alive together with Christ (by grace you have been saved) (Ephesians 2:4-5).

What a blessing to have a God who is "rich in mercy." His mercy operates as a taproot for our blessings of life in Christ Jesus.

God's mercy has also manifested itself at other critical junctures in His people's history. God's deliverance of Israel from Egyptian slavery was because of His merciful response to their cries of affliction (Exodus 3:7). It was mercy that moved God to deliver Israel from Babylonian captivity (Isaiah 49:13; Ezekiel 39:25). God's tenderheartedness moved Him to extend Hezekiah's life (2 Kings 20:5-6). Jesus' compassion stirred Him to heal the sick (e.g. Matthew 14:14; Mark 1:41). And in many other instances throughout Scripture, mercy can be seen as the driving force behind God's actions toward humanity. Noted scholar Jack Cottrell perhaps best sums up God's relation to this dimension of love: "God does not choose to be merciful; He is merciful."[43]

Longsuffering is probably the least discussed dimension of God's love, but I think we are all keenly aware of its importance. Thankfulness for God's patience with our weaknesses should frequently be offered up in our prayers.

Peter provided an excellent explanation of God's trait of longsuffering; "The Lord is not slow about His promise, as some count slowness, but is patient toward you, not wishing any to perish but for all to come to repentance" (2 Peter 3:9). Even though we may be prone to disobedience, our longsuffering God does not give up on us. He would prefer to give us grace than the judgment we deserve, so He exhibits undue patience with us. God's longstanding patience with Israel's continual disobedience in their pursuit of false gods and ill-treatment of the poor serves as an excellent example of His longsuffering. Nehemiah aptly spoke of God's patience toward defiant Israel; "However, You bore with them for many years, And admonished them by Your Spirit through Your prophets, Yet they would not give ear" (Nehemiah 9:30).

God's love in a nutshell – mercy saw humanity's suffering and stirred benevolence into action by offering Christ for our sins, which spurred on grace to extend forgiveness to an undeserving people. Longsuffering's hope of repentance seeks to keep grace extended and wrath at bay.

To help illustrate how the four aspects of God's love work harmoniously together, I would like to share with you a story by an unknown author titled the "The Waitress' Tip."

> When an ice cream sundae cost much less, a boy entered a coffee shop and sat at a table. A waitress put a glass of water in front of him. [He asked,] "How much is an ice cream sundae?"
>
> "Fifty cents," replied the waitress.
>
> The little boy pulled his hand out of his pocket and studied a number of coins in it. "How much is a dish of plain ice cream?" he inquired.
>
> Some people were now waiting for a table, and the waitress was impatient. "Thirty-five cents," she said angrily.
>
> The little boy again counted the coins. "I'll have the plain ice cream."
>
> The waitress brought the ice cream and walked away. The boy finished, paid the cashier, and departed.
>
> When the waitress came back, she swallowed hard at what she saw. There, placed neatly beside the empty dish, were two nickels and five pennies – her tip.

Money was not the object that kept the boy from the sundae he truly desired. His benevolent heart decided to look out for the waitress' welfare, and he chose something lesser for himself. The waitress did not deserve a tip, but the boy's gracious nature guided him to leave her one. Glares of impatience and an angry tone required the boy to show undue patience (longsuffering) with the annoyed waitress, yet somehow this boy saw through a scornful veneer to a heart that needed a compassionate gesture. To the waitress it was more than a gesture; it was a life-lesson I am sure she would not soon forget.

In its entirety, God's Word may be viewed as a love story between God and humanity. As God reached out in an attempt to rebuild a relationship with His wayward creation, He often used angels to administer His loving touch. It is to these angelic missions of love that we now turn to learn more about our affectionate God.

Chapter 5

Angels
and the Redemption Story

You have made him for a little while
lower than the angels ... And have
appointed him over the works
of Your hands (Hebrews 2:7).

My mother was a great southern cook. Bacon, eggs, grits, and toast with honey were a staple in the mornings. A typical dinner might consist of fried or barbecued chicken, pork chops, ham, stewed white beans, mashed potatoes and gravy, fried okra, fresh green beans, or greens. I still remember walking with mom by the edge of the woods at certain times of the year to pick poke greens for dinner. By today's standards much of this cuisine would not be considered too healthy, but my mom had a way of balancing our diets that kept us relatively trim. Of the many yummy things she cooked, her fried chicken trumped them all. Even the Colonel would have been envious.

After rolling waxed paper out on the kitchen counter, my mom then floured and applied her secret spices to the chicken. What a wonderful sound the chicken made when she placed it in the skillet. Time after time, she always had the oil at just the right temperature to create a light but never-too-crispy crust – truly mouthwatering. When she brought the prized chicken to the table, it would be on a platter with a paper towel under the chicken to absorb any excess oil. My mom gave my dad the thighs. She gave me the drumsticks, and for herself she took a breast. I always thought it was great that my mom loved the white meat, so I was able to have the moist dark meat. What a great blessing to have a mom who was a top-notch cook.

In her old age, my mother had been severely debilitated by rheumatoid arthritis. Because of her need for around-the-clock care, she eventually entered a nursing home, where she could receive the proper attention she needed. One evening I was visiting her when an attendant came in with her dinner. She had asked for chicken, but to my surprise the attendant placed before her a thigh and leg quarter. Because her fingers had become so badly disfigured by the arthritis, I cut up the chicken for her. While doing this I asked her why she had requested the dark meat, when all those years at home, she seemed to cherish the chicken breast. She told me that actually the dark meat had always been her favorite. She settled for the chicken breast because she wanted me and my dad to have "the best" pieces. Not only was I in shock; my heart began to break. All those years I benefited from a mother's sacrificial love and had not realized it. Setting aside her own preference, she silently placed the desires of her family first. This event taught me a very valuable life-lesson about *agape* love. From that point forward, I have tried to emulate this blessed character trait of my mother, though it has not always been easy. Yes, having a mom who was a wonderful cook is a great thing, but by no means does it compare to the blessings bestowed by a mother who demonstrates a sacrificial love for her family.

Of all God's traits, we exalt His sacrificial love above all others; and rightfully so, because what God has done for us through Christ Jesus is beyond amazing. But why does He care so much about us? With all our shortcomings you would expect God to give up on us. Nevertheless, because we bear His image, God must cherish the glorious potential that lies within us. To realize this potential is the tricky part. God must recreate a state of holiness within the human soul and provide us with the ability to sustain it. To accomplish such a great feat, Jesus entered the human realm to redeem us from the consequences of sin. Gospel preachers then spread this good news of God's redeeming love to the world. As God put into motion His redemption plan, He assured its success by strategically intervening with His holy angels. Through their involvement we can see the love of our Creator in action.

Birth Announcements

On May 25, 1961, President John F. Kennedy challenged America with the goal of landing humans on the Moon by the end of the decade. Historically, this was a monumental announcement. Excitement gripped the nation, and the country mobilized its resources to achieve this lofty goal. Seeing Neil Armstrong and Buzz Aldrin walking on the Moon in July 1969 made the world truly marvel at what had been accomplished by the U.S. Space Program.

Taking into account some of the more significant historic announcements, Kennedy's ranks up there with some of the best; yet, it pales in comparison to two declarations made by angels a couple millennia earlier. These angelic announcements did not come with the hoopla of going before a joint session of Congress. They came in two private sessions; one with a lowly carpenter and the other with the woman to whom he was betrothed. Throughout history, there have been no serious rivals to the angels' announcement that Mary would give birth to mankind's Savior, with the arguable exception of the angel's announcement that Jesus had risen from the grave. Jesus' birth announcements ushered in the initiation of mankind's redemption. In sending angels, God put His divine stamp on the upcoming events. Neither Mary nor Joseph wavered from accepting their new responsibilities, because the supernatural presence of an angel made it impossible to overlook God's divine direction.[44] Along with these two announcements, an angel also proclaimed the humble arrival of the Savior to some shepherds. All these angelic events serve to illuminate our understanding of God's love.

The first story we encounter in the New Testament is the birth announcement of Jesus to a bewildered Joseph (Matthew 1:18-25). Because of Mary's unexpected pregnancy, righteous Joseph wanted to "send her away secretly" and preclude bringing any disgrace upon her. To explain the extraordinary circumstances surrounding Mary's pregnancy, God sends an angel to appear in one of the shocked young man's dreams. This remarkable power of the angels has always fascinated me. Would it not be a useful ability to show up in someone else's dream? Maybe our kids would pay better attention to us if we emerged in their dreams in flames of fire authoritatively demanding, "Clean your room!" Or perhaps a gentler approach would be more appropriate – with soft whispers we could subliminally suggest, "Clean your room, clean your room, cleannn yourrr rooooom." In all seriousness, to appear in someone's dream-state and pass on a message would be an extremely complicated endeavor. Interfacing with the human brain to accomplish such a thing boggles the mind. A thorough understanding of how dreams work continues to escape today's scientists, but for our Master Designer, outfitting the angels with the ability to plug into human dreams was a piece of cake.

With the goal of encouraging Joseph to continue with his marriage plans, the angel informed him that Mary's child had been conceived by the Holy Spirit (Matthew 1:20). Can you imagine what Joseph must have been thinking prior to the angel's visit? "How could Mary have done this to me?" "Did she not realize what a wonderful husband I would have been?" While still dealing with the betrayal and grief, if someone then came to you and assured you that the Holy Spirit was responsible for Mary's pregnancy, would you believe it? Could you accept the fact that she was honored and blessed rather than unfaithful and disgraced? Oh, and by the way, you will be the earthly father of the Christ child. Considering the circumstances, this would be extremely hard to swallow. We have all heard some tall tales, but that one sounds like a doozy. You can see God's wisdom at work in sending an angel to explain the situation. Divine intervention would be required to convince Joseph of Mary's purity.

> The name *Jesus* means "*Yahweh* (God) is salvation" or "*Yahweh* saves" and describes His fundamental purpose for coming.[45]

The angel stated that Mary "will bear a Son; and you shall call His name Jesus, for He will save His people from their sins" (Matthew 1:21). The angel's declaration succinctly defines Jesus' ministry. He would provide spiritual salvation for His people from the corruption of sin. We think the onset of being a parent is daunting. How about the weighty responsibility Joseph and Mary now faced? They were to be the earthly parents of the Savior of all humanity!

Unlike Joseph's angelic experience, Mary encountered the angel Gabriel within the physical realm (Luke 1:26-38). Gabriel revealed that God, through the Holy Spirit, would create within her a holy offspring, the Son of God, and as in Joseph's dream, instruction was given that the child should be named Jesus, again indicating the child's Savior status. Upon greeting her, Gabriel referred to Mary as "favored one" (v. 28). I cannot imagine a greater honor to be given an individual than for God to request that you give birth and be a mother to His Son. You could imagine Mary internally saying, "No way, this just cannot be true; someone wake me up!" Even the angel knew the incredible nature of his proposition and assured Mary that nothing was "impossible with God" (v. 37). The heart of Mary that God obviously cherished became evident from her response to Gabriel; "Behold, the bond-slave of the Lord; may it be done to me according to your word" (v. 38; see also v. 48). Again we see the wisdom of God at work. To persuade Mary that such a remarkable scenario could occur, the visitation of divine Gabriel would leave no room for doubt to the authenticity and plausibility of the remarkable events that awaited her.

During his conversation with Mary, Gabriel told her that the child would fulfill the long-awaited promise of a Messiah who was to come from the line of David.

> He will be great and will be called the Son of the Most High; and the Lord God will give Him the throne of His father David; and He will reign over the house of Jacob forever, and His kingdom will have no end (Luke 1:32-33).

By indicating Jesus' lofty status, Gabriel attested to the fact that Jesus was the anointed one, whom the Old Testament prophets identified as the Savior and righteous King that would establish God's everlasting government.

God never ceases to amaze me. Disillusioned by today's self-seeking culture, I might have expected Him to announce the arrival of His new born Son to the most prestigious kings and religious leaders of the day. Wrong! God sought out some humble isolated shepherds to make His grand announcement. Following His pattern, you would then expect the birth notice to be carried out in a low-key manner. Bamboozled again! With the heart of an overjoyed Father, God proclaimed His good news in a joyous, impressive display of the supernatural (Luke 2:8-14). In the dead of night, as the shepherds watched over their sheep in the fields of Bethlehem, an angel dramatically appeared, and a glorious light suddenly enveloped them. Almost

Angels are often associated with light in Scripture, but Luke 2:9 may give us a hint as to its source. As the angel stood before the shepherds, "the glory of the Lord shone around them." The light could denote God's presence (e.g. Exodus 40:34-38), but the text does not otherwise suggest that. Perhaps the brilliant light emanated from the angel because he had just come from the presence of God, similar to when Moses' face shined after leaving God's presence (Exodus 34:29-35).

instantaneously, the shepherds' quiet, routine night was transformed into a terrifying, life-changing affair. God's herald immediately soothed the shepherds' fears and then rocked the world
with the following proclamation:

> ... Do not be afraid; for behold, I bring you good news of
> a great joy which shall be for all the people; for today in the
> city of David there has been born for you a Savior, who is
> Christ the Lord. And this will be a sign for you: you will find
> a baby wrapped in cloths and lying in a manger. (vv. 10-12).

Gabriel's promise had been fulfilled. Through a human womb
the Messiah entered the earthly realm. The Greek term "Christ" that
the angel used is equivalent to the Hebrew word for messiah, thus
the anointed One had arrived. With the announcement of the Savior's birth, heaven's joy could not be contained. Suddenly, a multi-
tude of the heavenly hosts joined the sole angel and the shepherds.
As witnesses to the love that flowed from heaven, the angels joyously praised God for His gracious work (Luke 2:13-14). With such
heavenly motivation, hesitation was not an option. The shepherds
made a beeline straight to Bethlehem to see the Christ child.

Even though these announcements momentarily placed the angels on center stage, this event was not about them. Their supernatural presence served the purpose of drawing mankind's
attention to the unfolding of God's gracious plan of redemption.
God sent these angels, and His authority accompanied their divine mission of love. In all three birth announcements, the angels'
mission involved pointing their listeners to the Savior. Joseph became aware that Mary would give birth to the Savior. Gabriel told
Mary that she would be the mother of the Savior. The angel directly pointed the shepherds to the Savior in Bethlehem. Likewise,
through these nativity stories, we too have been pointed to the
Savior. But we must ask ourselves one question, have we done
our share of "pointing" others to the Savior?

Do you remember the first time you ever held a newborn baby? What a fascinating experience! Their soft, smooth skin and fine wisps of hair irresistibly beckoned our touch. As trusting eyes wondrously met our own, our hearts began to melt and would even compel the manliest of men to start communicating in a strange new tongue – baby talk. Enticed by little bitty hands, we uncontrollably offered a finger to be grasped by these delicate creatures. Helpless and vulnerable, this magnificent, tender child was totally dependent on human care. Angels declared that God entered our world in such a form and could be found lying in a manger.

Each time we encounter someone with a baby, an opportunity avails itself to mention how God chose to come into this world in such a vulnerable state. Humanity's Savior utterly depended on the care of loving parents; roles Mary and Joseph cherished and fulfilled. The tenderness of this part of the redemption story draws one to reflect on God's wondrous plan. Take a lesson from the angels and avail yourselves of such opportunities, joyously pointing others to the work of love in Christ Jesus. Let this message dwell in their hearts. God's life-giving power resides in this good news.

> By this the love of God was manifested in us, that God has sent His only begotten Son into the world so that we might live through Him. In this is love, not that we loved God, but that He loved us and sent His Son to be the propitiation [appeasement] for our sins. (1 John 4:9-10).

Spread of the Redemption Story

Have you ever been selected to participate in an activity not knowing what your role would be? This happened to me a few times during my career at NASA. Special teams were frequently formed for specific periods of time to investigate something of interest to the Agency. After the initial meeting with the team's leader, you would most likely understand your role, but sometimes it evolved over the life of the project. In a similar manner, the apostles had to be dumbfounded on how their roles would evolve after

Christ's ascension. Yes, Jesus said they would be His witnesses (Acts 1:8), but can you imagine what the apostles must have been thinking as Jesus was lifted up and disappeared into a cloud (v. 9)? "What can we alone possibly do?" "If the Son of God could not escape the clutches of our religious leaders, how does God suppose we can succeed?" "Without the leadership of Jesus, how can an improbable band of fishermen, tax collectors, etc., accomplish anything?" "What is God's plan, and what does He expect of us?" "What's next?"

I believe angels shared the apostles' quandary. On the flipside of reality, envision the scene in heaven. As the apostles watched Jesus' ascension from the earth, the angels watched His grand entrance into heaven. This was a once-in-an-eternity event; excitement surely filled the air (or perhaps ether). But after the festivities, and with Jesus exalted to the right hand of His Father, the angels likewise probably wondered – "What's next?"

Angels, unlike God, are not all-knowing (Mark 13:32; 1 Peter 1:12). Peter attested to this when he told the recipients of his first letter that they were privileged to have the gospel message preached to them before it had been revealed to the angels, and most assuredly the heavenly hosts desired to understand how God's redemption story would unfold (vv. 10-12; also see Ephesians 3:8-10). Like the apostles, the angels too waited for God's next step. They must have wondered if they would continue to play a role in humanity's redemption. Would their unique God-given powers be used in this gracious work? In Acts, Luke gave us a glimpse into how God intervened with these mighty beings in the spreading of His story of love.

God wasted no time in utilizing the angels as He put into motion the next steps of His plan. While the apostles gazed into the sky at their ascending Lord like space enthusiasts watching a Shuttle launch, two angelic visitors clad in white suddenly appeared in their midst (Acts 1:9-10). God knew these dedicated men would be crushed at Jesus' departure, so He sent angels to remind them of a promise (Matthew 16:27) Jesus previously shared with them;

"Men of Galilee, why do you stand looking into the sky? This Jesus, who has been taken up from you into heaven, will come in just the same way as you have watched Him go into heaven" (Acts 1:11). Reassurance from God that He was still in control provided the apostles courage to stay the course as they headed down an unknown and evolving new pathway.

Equipped with the Holy Spirit at Pentecost, the apostles became emboldened, enlightened, and skilled gospel preachers with miraculous powers attesting to their God-given mission. Initially they took God's good news of redemption to the Jews. However, because thousands had come to believe in Jesus through the apostle's teachings, along with the people's attraction to their miracles, the Jewish leaders became enraged with jealousy and threw the apostles in jail (Acts 5:17-18). Little did they know that they were trying to put out a dry brush fire with gasoline. God responded to this threat against the spread of His redeeming love by sending an angel that night to conduct a jailbreak. The details are sketchy, but it appears that the angel miraculously opened locked gates and led the apostles past unaware prison guards (vv. 19, 23). After liberating them, the angel directed the encouraged band to "[g]o, stand and speak to the people in the temple the whole message of this Life" (v. 20).

No longer convicts but now convicted, the apostles' angelic encounter unquestionably left them with the confidence that they should press on with their preaching mission. Even with the looming threat of being punished, the apostles' obedience was immediate; they entered the temple grounds and taught the people.

Prisoners of their own delusions of grandeur, the religious leaders' hardheadedness and hardheartedness kept them from recognizing God's intervention in the release of the apostles. When the defiant apostles were brought before the Council again, the high priest chided them for teaching in the name of Jesus. Having been emboldened by the angel, the apostles confidently responded, "We must obey God rather than men" (Acts 5:29). Note that they did not say, "We must obey the angel who delivered us."

They equated the angel's words with that of God's. With divine assurance from God that they were doing His will, the apostles could take a flogging yet still rejoice because they suffered for Jesus' name (vv. 40-41). In the not too distant past, these men were afraid of the religious leaders' wrath, but now these divinely inspired apostles kept on keeping on; "And every day, in the temple and from house to house, they kept right on teaching and preaching Jesus as the Christ" (v. 42)

Sometimes a little reassurance goes a long way to instill confidence in a young Christian. I remember a dear brother years ago who told me how impressed he was with my spiritual growth and that I was on the right track in life. This happened at a crucial time for me, because I was hurting over an ugly political situation that had occurred within my church. This brother lifted me up, and his words of encouragement renewed my zeal. It was a "keep on keeping on" moment for me. Words of encouragement should flow naturally from a Christian, especially leaders. In no uncertain terms, it is an indication that you are spiritually on the right track. Christians who have a propensity for criticism are most likely spiritually immature or perhaps even have a corrupted spirituality. Let me incite you to act like an angel; reassure and encourage your Christian family. It will embolden needful brothers and sisters to greater things.

As Acts continues to disclose the church's development, the Holy Spirit-equipped preachers made considerable headway with the Jews in Judea. But how did God spur them to move beyond these familiar borders, as well as motivate them to offer His plan of salvation to the despised Gentiles? Several dramatic events occurred that started to push the proclamation of the gospel beyond Judea, such as the persecution of the disciples and conversion of Paul (Acts 8:4; 9:15), but several obstacles still stood in the way of achieving these two goals. Therefore, God also enlisted angels in two separate situations to provide a divine nudge in order to bring together a gospel preacher and a seeking heart.[46]

Have you ever come across individuals who enthusiastically soaked up everything you taught them from God's Word? Teaching others who genuinely have such fervor is extremely gratifying. I spent some time mentoring two young men, John "Beef" Branard and Keith Merritt. We went on what I like to call "God talks" from time to time. Our "God talks" were simply short trips to a nearby town filled with conversations on biblical topics and plenty of barbeque. When my son was home from college, he enjoyed these excursions as well. I deliberately chose to take these guys out of town because it would necessitate longer drives. I knew that they would be forced to talk to me for an extended length of time or else go nuts. Talking to me about spiritual topics never seemed to be a problem for those two young men. They were not only attentive to what I shared with them, but they asked many intriguing spiritual questions. It proved to be a formational time for all of us; and boy, could they put a hurtin' on the barbeque!

Because of the persecution of Christians in Jerusalem, Philip went on an evangelistic mission into Samaria (Acts 8), where low and behold he came across multitudes of Beef and Keith's; that is, there were many people who were genuinely attentive to Philip's preaching about Christ. Preachers would call this "fertile evangelistic ground." After converting many Samaritans, Philip started back to Jerusalem, and along the way he continued to preach in the Samaritan villages. But our unpredictable God decided to alter Philip's plans; "But an angel of the Lord spoke to Philip saying, 'Get up and go south to the road that descends from Jerusalem to Gaza.' (This is a desert road)" (v. 26). Without this divine direction, Philip would have likely continued to concentrate his efforts in the fertile villages of Samaria, rather than go to a desolate place which seemed unsuitable for preaching the gospel.[47] Angelic direction was a sign to Philip that God's authority stood behind this new plan of attack, so he immediately headed south. God's strategic wisdom started to unfold when Philip came upon an Ethiopian treasurer who was returning to his homeland after having been to Jerusalem to worship (vv. 27-39). With a remarkable display of

God's providence, the Ethiopian "just happened" to be reading prophecy from Isaiah dealing with the Savior's redeeming death. Not only did Philip lead him to a decision to be baptized for the forgiveness of his sins, but the Ethiopian then took the gospel message of God's love to a new continent.

In the conversion narrative about Cornelius (Acts 10), we can clearly see that God confronted the longstanding Jewish prejudice against the Gentiles. To accept the Gentiles as joint heirs to God's grace was a troubling proposition for the Jews. Even God's apostles were tainted by this prejudicial poison. With the need to radically reshape some attitudes, God resorted to extraordinary means to demonstrate His commitment that Christ died for all.

Cornelius was a Roman centurion. Luke described him as "a devout man and one who feared God with all his household, and gave many alms to the Jewish people and prayed to God continually" (Acts 10:2). God chose an excellent first candidate for conversion, because even the Jews recognized Cornelius' godly ways. Regrettably though, this fell way short of what needed to occur; God's stamp of authority needed to be unmistakably visible on any change of status involving the Gentiles. While praying in the middle of the afternoon, Cornelius unexpectedly had a visitor. In shining garments, an angel suddenly appeared before him (vv. 3, 30). Startled by the supernatural vision, Cornelius' eyes were glued to the dazzling figure. The angel honored him by testifying to God's high regard for his godly ways; "Your prayers and alms have ascended as a memorial before God" (v. 4). After listening to the angel's message, Cornelius needed to act on faith. Peter was to be brought to Cornelius' home to share an important message with him (vv. 5, 22). From Cornelius' perspective, Peter represented a leader from a radical Jewish sect; to be associated with him would not be pleasing to the Jews he had been supporting.

Considering Peter's stubborn disposition, I am not so sure he would have been too keen on this plan. Without God's intervention, you could imagine Peter's response to some "unclean" Gentiles appearing at his door requesting that he come with them to another city, "I don't think so!" Although, Peter's ears would have certainly perked up when he heard that Cornelius "was divinely directed by a holy angel to send for you" (Acts 10: 22). Yet would this be enough to convince Peter? To assure that God had Peter's attention, He also conveyed in three separate visions that the Gentiles should now be considered clean (vv. 9-16). God even directly intervened through the Holy Spirit by commanding Peter to go with Cornelius' servants "without misgivings" (vv. 19-20). Kind of reminds me of a coach who repeatedly blows his shrill whistle to garner his team's attention. Such shrill attention-grabbers would not go unnoticed by Peter.

Peter appeared to grasp God's message. He went with the servants to Cornelius' home, and when they arrived Peter made the following statement; "I most certainly understand now that God is not one to show partiality, but in every nation the man who fears Him and does what is right is welcome to Him" (Acts 10:34-35). In one final act, God leaves no room for interpretation of His intentions. While Peter preached the gospel to Cornelius and his household, the Holy Spirit came upon them as it had the apostles at Pentecost. Cornelius and his household were then baptized. The level of God's intercession spoke to the deeply entrenched abhorrence the Jews had for the Gentiles, while at the same time demonstrated the power of God's love for all humanity.

In both the Philip and Cornelius' stories, God utilized an angel to facilitate bringing together a gospel preacher and someone seeking Him. This resulted in new avenues being opened up to spread God's message. But do the angels' roles in these two stories provide us with any practical insight for our service to God today? In mulling over this question, it is important to note what the angels "did not do." They did not preach the gospel; that is our responsibility. Paul explains that God entrusts the redeemed with the spread of the redemption story (2 Corinthians 5:18-19). We are God's ambassadors to the world for Christ (v. 20); but to effectively accomplish the goal of spreading the gospel story, God's love must first be infused in our hearts. This love enables us to see the helpless and lost world that we live in and to identify those who need this message of grace to make their lives right with God. When our hearts are full of His mercy, we can extend the gospel to them in a productive manner. What greater love can we express to others than to assist them in receiving the eternal blessings Christ brings through His gospel?

What the angels "did do" was to stimulate others to carry out God's desires. Sometimes we may fall short in our abilities or resources to help others, but that does not mean we should throw in the towel and quit on them. We can be a "stimulator." By encouraging our brothers and sisters to come alongside us in a good work, we may be able to collectively meet the dire needs of others. This falls right in line with the thought expressed by the writer of Hebrews; "[A]nd let us consider how to stimulate one another to love and good deeds" (Hebrews 10:24). Involving our brothers and sisters will not only help us successfully accomplish a good work, but it will also provide them an opportunity to grow by participating in works of love.

A Time for Angels to Rejoice

God is possessive; once we become one of His own, He wants to keep us. Yet He also cherishes liberty, and if we choose to go astray He won't stop us. Scripture emphasizes the tremendous value God still places on the wayward sinner. In the parables of the lost sheep, lost coin, and prodigal son, the characters who recovered what was lost wanted others to rejoice with them (Luke 15:1-32). These characters represent God and illustrate the overwhelming joy He feels when a lost sinner returns to Him. God's love for those reaching out for forgiveness is most aptly expressed in the scene when the prodigal son returns; "But while he was still a long way off, his father saw him and felt compassion for him, and ran and embraced him and kissed him" (v. 20). We definitely need to get our arms around this verse. Jesus has blessed us with a powerful picture of His compassionate Father. When a lost soul (the prodigal son) turns to God (the father) with the intent of leaving their sin behind, He is overcome with compassion. He cannot reach us fast enough. He takes hold of us and welcomes us home with hugs and kisses. We are His creation. He knows our potential and values what we can become through His beloved Son. Yes, we will be embarrassed of our past and tears will flow; but our hearts will quickly melt in His loving embrace. We have forgiveness. What love! Thank you, Father.

God does not stop there – He celebrates our redemption. Luke tells us that the return of one of God's own is an emotional event; "In the same way, I tell you, there is joy in the presence of the angels of God over one sinner who repents" (Luke 15:10). I wish Luke would have shared how the angels expressed their joy. Assuming the angels symbolized God's servants in the parable of the prodigal son, perhaps they were merrily cooking up a heavenly feast, striking up the angel chorus, and dancing with the stars. Angelic rejoicing may be amusing to think about, but the intent of these parables is to point out God's festive mood when a wayward Christian chooses to return to Him. Along with the restorative power of God's redeeming love, God's accompanying celebratory spirit serves to instill value in the one experiencing a welcome home. God loves us. When His redeeming love flows out, it is a time of tremendous joy; a joy to be shared. Joy angels cannot resist. Can we?

One Sunday, I remember a celebration of monumental proportions at the church I was attending. An individual from a long-standing family of the congregation turned their life over to Christ. Upon completion of the worship service droves of people streamed to the front of the auditorium. Hugs, well-wishes, tears, and comments of pride were showered upon this new Christian. In stark contrast to this, the next Sunday an unknown woman also went forward and turned her life over to Christ. This time only a couple of church members took the time to come forward to congratulate her. Everyone else either turned around and left, or they broke up into their cliques. I was overtaken by two sets of emotions. On the one hand

I was happy for this new sister, but at the same time my heart was breaking for her. Where was the celebration?

Staying Power of God's Love

Paul let the church in Rome know that not only was there victory in Jesus, but that victory had the staying power of God's love behind it.

> For I am convinced that neither death, nor life, nor angels, nor principalities, nor things present, nor things to come, nor powers, nor height, nor depth, nor any other created thing, will be able to separate us from the love of God, which is in Christ Jesus our Lord (Romans 8:38-39).

Some suggest that the "angels" in this verse should be classified as evil because they want to separate us from God's love.[48] However, this is unlikely to be Paul's intent. The New Testament writers typically include a descriptor if the angel is not holy (e.g., Matthew 25:41; Revelation 12:7).[49] Paul appears to be saying that in all the created dimensions, nothing can separate us from God. Thus the terms "angels" and "principalities" (Romans 8:38-39) would be covering the entire spiritual realm, i.e. the spectrum of good and evil angels.[50]

These wonderful words hold a powerful reassuring message of God's commitment to us. Nothing across the entire spectrum of human, spiritual, temporal, or physical dimensions has the ability to separate us from God's love. Not even the mightiest of God's holy angels or the most devious satanic messenger can wedge us away from God's loving embrace. This promise is not groundless rhetoric but was demonstrated in the cross. Not even God's Son was spared because of His love for us (v. 32). God's love through

Jesus Christ allows us to overwhelmingly conquer anything that attempts to separate us from Him (v. 37).

Throughout life, our faith will be assaulted by a diverse array of harmful things. We need to hold fast to our knowledge that not an enemy on the battlefield, a spiteful boss or co-worker, an unforgiving relative, a terminal illness, a godless political official, a corrupt media outlet, a financial crisis, or a spiritual being has the power to remove us from the graces of God's love in Christ Jesus. Externals are powerless; internally, you have a choice. It is in your hands. God's grace is for the believing heart to accept, be nurtured by, and cherish; then nothing, not even an ominous angel, can take away this gift of God.

Questions

1. Can you recall a time in your life when someone sacrificially did something for you? What do you think about that person? What did you learn from that situation?

2. Why do you think God has gone to such great extremes to have a relationship with us? What can we learn about Him through His redemptive work?

3. Have you ever considered the evangelistic aspects of the nativity stories? How might you use those stories to reach out to others and draw them to Jesus?

4 Why do you think it was appropriate for God to use angels during the in-breaking and spread of the redemption story? What are some other means God could have used? What advantages would using angels have over the other means you identified?

5. What was the central focus of the angels' announcements that surrounded Jesus' birth? What significance does this have for us today?

6. Are their groups of people that you have a tough time reaching out to? What specifically impedes you? Does the story of Cornelius help you with this? How?

7. Are there currently any opportunities where you could help someone in need by stimulating a brother or sister to help?

8. Can you recall a time when you were overwhelmed with joy when you found something that was lost? Do you have this same kind of joy when someone you know comes (or returns) to Christ? What are some ways you can rejoice with others when people come or return to Christ? Have you encountered a similar situation, as described in this chapter, when more people rejoiced with one new Christian over another? What can be done to improve these situations?

9. How does God keep external things from having the power to separate us from Him? In what areas of your life does this provide you encouragement?

10. How is sharing Jesus an expression of mercy and *agape* love? What are some ways you can break the ice with others to share the gospel with them?

Chapter 6

Agents of
God's Compassion

The LORD answered
the angel who was speaking with me
with gracious words, comforting words (Zechariah 1:13).

Have you ever met anyone who was drawn to the down-and-out? I have a brother in Christ who has a gift from God that would scare the stuffing out of most of us. My friend Steve Ruse is attracted to a segment of society that most people would consider outcasts. Even a good number of churches hesitate reaching out to them. But Steve does, because to him, they are God's children who are in dire need of help. Steve's compassionate desire to serve these people consequently stirs up his wife Andria's merciful nature as well. He has brought her alongside him in many of his benevolent endeavors. Without her involvement, many of these compassionate projects would have been doomed to failure. They have reached out and assisted society's needy individuals in what most would consider extreme ways. Recovering alcoholics and drug addicts, those recently released from jail, underprivileged youth, single parent families, and the impoverished all have benefited from this noble couple's mercy.

Of the many compassionate causes that Steve and Andria have undertaken, there is one that truly stands above the rest in their commitment to helping others. Steve is a reformed alcoholic and successfully made it through Alcoholic Anonymous' recovery program many years ago. During his recovery process, the plight of others, whose struggles he can deeply identify with, started pricking at his heart. Just before I met Steve, he had become a Christian, and his awareness of others' needs seemed to become a consuming fire within him. We started a home Bible study; and as you might guess, there was often a diverse group of individuals in attendance each week.

To help you grasp how Steve approaches life, if you looked up the word "unexpected" in the dictionary, his smiling face would be right next to the definition. For Steve, the unexpected is the norm. However, in this one instance Steve moved out of the unexpected into the shocking category. Prior to a Bible study one week, he informed me that he and Andria had embarked on a new endeavor that caused my jaw to almost drop off its hinges – they invited someone into their home to die. Yes, I said die. While working with AA, Steve had come across a man who had been diagnosed with terminal cancer. This individual had nowhere to go and no one to turn to. Steve and Andria's heart went out to him, so they brought him into their home where he could be lovingly cared for and allowed him to pass on with dignity. Even though they had two little children of their own to care for, they simply could not deny compassion's call. What love!

God's compassion often catches us off guard. We tend to associate compassion with Jesus and justice with God. When God's longsuffering wanes and is displaced by his wrath, we our confronted with some harsh judgments against those who have stood in rebellion against Him. Stories of banishment, floods, plagues, death, fire and brimstone, defeat, and exile may become our focus and incorrectly skew our understanding of God. However, the entire Bible is filled with stories of God's compassion, and a proper reading of His Word will show humanity's story is primarily framed in God's love and mercy. We have already looked at how God's compassionate nature has reached out to humanity through the work of Jesus and spread of the gospel, but what about all the trials we face in our lives; does God care? Is He concerned about us when we are being mistreated or suffering? Is He ever constrained in His ability to respond compassionately? In several instances in Scripture, we can see God responding compassionately to others by sending angels to address their problems. These stories serve to highlight God's concern for our welfare.

Hagar's Angelic Encounters

Genesis provides two intriguing stories when God intervened with heavenly assistance in the travails of Sarah's maid, Hagar. The first account speaks to Sarah's desperation in providing Abraham with offspring (Genesis 16:1-14). Knowing her childbearing days were behind her, Sarah came up with a precarious scheme to give Abraham children despite her age. Her plan was to have children through Hagar, so Sarah suggested that Abraham have relations with her maid servant. I doubt that this suggestion would be concocted by our wives today. Sarah's plan appeared to be coming together when Hagar conceived, but then an unanticipated result occurred – Hagar started to despise Sarah. You can imagine Hagar's thoughts on the matter, "How dare Sarah! This is my child with Abraham. No way will this child be construed as hers." Of course Sarah, in turn, treated Hagar harshly; so Hagar fled into the wilderness. It appears Sarah never consulted God about her plan; and as we all know, human reasoning can be a recipe for disaster.

God knew Hagar was with child and to be alone in the wilderness would leave her open to all sorts of perils. God sent the angel of the Lord to comfort her and give her guidance.

> Then the angel of the LORD said to her, "Return to your mistress, and submit yourself to her authority." Moreover, the angel of the LORD said to her, "I will greatly multiply your descendants so that they will be too many to count." The angel of the LORD said to her further, "Behold, you are with child, and you shall bear a son; And you shall call

his name Ishmael, Because the LORD has given heed to
your affliction" (Genesis 16:9-11).

The first time the term *angel* occurs in God's Word is in this
story. God does not choose Adam or Eve, Noah, or even Abraham or Sarah to meet the initial heavenly messenger. God selected
an Egyptian servant girl, whose descendants will never be a part of
Israel, to be the first beneficiary of the oft mentioned angel of the
Lord.[51] I am sure the original Hebrew readers of this story would
have shaken their heads in amazement at how broad God's compassion extends. Even today, I believe we may tend to overlook
many instances in which God's mercy is being administered.

While attending the Harding University Graduate School of Religion, I met a young woman who worked for Agape Ministries in
Memphis, Tennessee, ministering to homeless, unwed pregnant
women. What a calling! If God's mercies can seek out a pregnant
slave girl in the wilderness some four thousand years ago, why not
impoverished, pregnant women in the urban areas of America
today? It is just another wilderness we humans become lost in. We
need to pray for God's mercy-givers that work with individuals in
such dire circumstances. God's compassions are not restricted to
our churches.

Several items in this narrative speak to God's concern for
Hagar. First, the angel of the Lord directed her back to Sarah
where she would be safe. Second, the messenger assured Hagar
that the child she was carrying would be successfully delivered
and become the father of a great nation. Third, the angel stated
that God noted and acted on her affliction. Fourth, her son was to
be named Ishmael, which means "God hears." Her son's name
would memorialize God's merciful awareness of her plight. "God
hears" – what great hope that brings. We will explore this theme
further in Chapter 7.

Unfortunately, another thing the angel of the Lord predicted
was that Ishmael would be cantankerous (Genesis 16:12), and this
very trait propagated a later incident where Hagar again found

herself in the wilderness in a desperate situation (21:9-21). Because Sarah caught the young teenager Ishmael mocking her newborn son, Isaac, she had Abraham begrudgingly banish Hagar and
her son from their presence. After a short time, their water ran
out, and Hagar gave up hope that God's former promise concerning Ishmael would ever come true.

> [S]he left the boy under one of the bushes. Then she
> went and sat down opposite him, about a bowshot away,
> for she said, "Do not let me see the boy die." And she sat
> opposite him, and lifted up her voice and wept (vv. 15-16).

God heard the boy crying, and the angel of God called out
from heaven to Hagar asking,

> "What is the matter with you, Hagar? Do not fear, for
> God has heard the voice of the lad where he is. Arise, lift
> up the lad, and hold him by the hand, for I will make a great
> nation of him" (vv. 17-18).

With divine assistance, Hagar's eyes were opened to a nearby
well of water, which certainly saved them from an excruciating
death of dehydration.

When my son was about twelve years old, he somehow con-
tracted salmonella. The loss of fluids devastated my vibrant young-
ster's body, and he looked like an emaciated AIDS victim. What a
horrifying sight for a parent to behold! I still have burned into my
mind the image of my son's ravaged frame when he tried to stand
up by his hospital bed one night. I understand Hagar's pain and
why she could not bear seeing her son in such a condition.

This moving scene in the wilderness brings to light God's tenderheartedness. Again "God heard" (Genesis 21:17); this time it
was the cries of a young boy that stirred His merciful nature. God
compassionately responded by propelling the angel of God into
action to calm Hagar's fears. I love the tender language the angel

used upon directing Hagar to care for her son; "lift up the lad, and hold him by the hand" (v. 18). Immediately after saying this, God opened her eyes to the life-giving water that was unknowingly within her grasp. Today, God gives us the ability to open the eyes of a parched world to a new source of water. But unlike Hagar's well, the spiritual drink we can introduce them to has *eternal* life-giving quality (John 4:14).

Angelic Cooking for Elijah

If you came up with your top ten favorite Bible stories, I am sure the sacrifice contest between Elijah and the 450 prophets of Baal would show up on many of your lists (1 Kings 18:20-40). Tired of Israel's fickle allegiance of what deity to follow, Elijah states, "If the LORD is God, follow Him; but if Baal, follow him" (v. 21). To settle the matter, Elijah proposed a challenge. The prophets of Baal would offer a sacrifice to their god, and Elijah would offer a sacrifice to Jehovah God. Both would then call on the name of their god, and the one who answered with fire would be acknowledged as the true God.

Excitement gripped the prophets of Baal. An opportunity had finally availed itself for them to potentially humiliate their despised rival Elijah, while impressively demonstrating the power of their god, Baal. As they laid their sacrifice on the cold altar they constructed, their confidence had to soar, because 450 devoted prophets of the mighty Baal should bring fire upon the sacrifice in no time. They called out to Baal with great enthusiasm, leaping around the altar ready to be warmed by their god's victorious flames. However, as the morning hours dwindled away, only cold emanated from the altar's stones. At noon Elijah mocked them, "Call out with a loud voice, for he is a god; either he is occupied or gone aside, or is on a journey, or perhaps he is asleep and needs to be awakened" (1 Kings 18:27). In modern day sports lingo, Elijah taunted them with a little "smack talk." Enraged by such insults, zeal returned to Baal's prophets, and they started crying out with loud voices and cutting themselves with swords in an attempt to usher in Baal's fire. They thought that surely with such passionate pleas and devotion

Baal would hear them. To these inept prophets, no answer came. The expected fire from above had been replaced by the cool of the evening and cold stares from all the people.

Elijah then proceeded to prepare his sacrifice as the people curiously watched, wondering if this lone prophet would also make a fool of himself. He repaired God's altar, dug a trench around it, set the sacrifice on it, and then utterly drenched it with water. He then humbly approached God in prayer and received a response that must have startled even him:

> "O LORD, the God of Abraham, Isaac and Israel, today let it be known that You are God in Israel and that I am Your servant and I have done all these things at Your word. Answer me, O LORD, answer me, that this people may know that You, O LORD are God, and that You have turned their heart back again." Then the fire of the LORD fell and consumed the burnt offering and the wood and the stones and the dust, and licked up the water that was in the trench (1 Kings 18:36-38).

Now you see why this story sneaks on many of our top ten lists. Elijah must have been on cloud nine. God answered him in a powerful way; the people believed that the Lord is God, and the now "false" prophets were slain. The text implies that even King Ahab silently witnessed the event and was to join the sacrificial meal (v. 41). Because of this exciting turn of events, Elijah was surely thinking, "What a great victory for the Lord! Perhaps now my soul can be at peace because Israel's waywardness must certainly be at its end."

When Ahab rejoined his wife, Queen Jezebel, in Jezreel, he told her what Elijah had done. Idolatrous Jezebel could not stand for such sacrilege against her dearly-loved Baal. Evil hearts calculate evil, and hers immediately concocted a plan of vengeance. She sent a messenger to Elijah to deliver her intent to murder him within twenty-four hours (1 Kings 19:1-2).

Elijah knew this wicked woman meant business, and she had the army of Israel at her disposal. Fear gripped him, so he fled for his life into the wilderness. Alone, exhausted, distraught, Elijah's faith was shaken to its core. This righteous man was so despondent that he asked God to take his life; "It is enough; now, O Lord, take my life, for I am not better than my fathers" (1 Kings 19:4). What a reversal! On the top of the world in one moment and wallowing in the mire in the next; Elijah believed that he could not go on.

Kind of reminds me of hurricane and tornado victims; one day you are enjoying life in the comfort of your home, and then in an instant nature's destructive forces introduce you to homelessness and chaos. Because I have lived in Florida most of my life, I am familiar with running from hurricanes, although I have never lost my home. I have only had to put up with fallen trees, flooding and loss of power. I remember a number of years ago when a powerful hurricane loomed off our coast. My wife had already gone inland, while I hurriedly gathered up the last of our most precious belongings. After luring our dalmatian into the front seat of my truck, it was time to "get out of Dodge"; but I stood frozen, staring at our home. Tears filled my eyes as I recalled the many memories experienced in this wonderful home. I thought I had seen the last of it. Such moments help you appreciate the plight some people experience in life.

Faced with such evil, Elijah turned inward. God had just performed one of the most astounding miracles documented in Scripture, but to Elijah it must have seemed like eons ago. Elijah's words reveal that the memory of God's miraculous power had been pushed aside by his current concerns; " ... for I am not better than my fathers" (1 Kings 19:4). I've always wanted to holler back through the centuries at Elijah and say, "Remember God! Look at what He just did. Lean on His power." However, when dread overtakes us, we all have a tendency to lean on our own resources. Whether Elijah was better than his fathers was irrelevant. God should be sought in such circumstances, but it may require us to relinquish the control we so richly cherish.

Up to this point, God's beloved prophet had only responded to Jezebel's messenger, so God now countered with His own messenger as an initial step in restoring Elijah's faith.[52] In a merciful gesture God twice sent an angel to address the ailing prophet's physical needs before he attempted to take on his spiritual failings.

> He lay down and slept under a juniper tree; and behold, there was an angel touching him, and he said to him, "Arise, eat." Then he looked and behold, there was at his head a bread cake baked on hot stones, and a jar of water. So he ate and drank and lay down again. The angel of the LORD came again a second time and touched him and said, "Arise, eat, because the journey is too great for you." So he arose and ate and drank, and went in the strength of that food forty days and forty nights to Horeb, the mountain of God (1 Kings 19:5-8).

Instead of receiving his death wish, Elijah awakened to a breakfast prepared by an angel. Reminds me of making pancakes when camping; the aroma produced by hotcakes cooking in the morning air is hard to beat, but I am sure those "angel cakes" smelled especially delicious.

When we become depressed, good nourishment is important, but it is when we are least likely to pay attention to our nutritional needs. That is why it is so important for the church to rise up and prepare meals for those who are grieving. I remember how much that meant to me at the death of both my parents. God caringly saw to the physical needs of His prophet. On this angelic food, Elijah journeyed for forty days to meet God at Mount Horeb, where the Lord spiritually prepared him to undertake a new mission.

On first glance, Elijah's angelic encounters appear to be about meeting his physical needs. However, it does contain a valuable spiritual component, one that required Elijah to reflect on the situation. God had not left him. He was not alone. You can imagine Elijah's thoughts; "God does care about me; He sent one of His holy angels to see to my needs." Such an insight would spiritually strengthen him because of the realization that God cared for him.

God also expects us to show concern for one another. It may not be with bread cakes and water, but nonetheless He expects us to reach out in love. Early on in my Christian walk, I struggled with the command to love one another. How could God command such a thing? I wanted to love others, but my experience had been that love was developmental and did not happen overnight, so how could God demand that I love someone else? On top of that, we must admit that some people are not very lovable. Loving others appeared to require more of me than the self-discipline needed to overcome some of my vices; the heart was involved (of course I later came to realize the heart was involved with many of my vices as well). Yet, Jesus specifically points out love's importance to His disciples:

> A new commandment I give to you, that you love one another, even as I have loved you, that you also love one another. By this all men will know that you are My disciples, if you have love for one another (John 13:34-35).

Demonstrated love was to be the yardstick by which the world could distinguish Christians.

Our contemporary understanding of love may clutter our thinking in regard to Christ's commandment. When thinking of love, we tend to default to the notion of intimacy or fondness, such as between husband and wife, mother and daughter, or two close friends. However, Jesus was referring to *agape* love. A love that is benevolent and sacrificial. Upon seeing the needful circumstances of others, *agape* love compassionately moves us to come to their aid. Paul sums up this quality in a statement he made to the Philippians:

> Do nothing from selfishness or empty conceit, but with humility of mind regard one another as more important than yourselves; do not merely look out for your own per-

sonal interests, but also for the interests of others
(Philippians 2:3-4).

Paul went on to explain that it was this quality that motivated
Jesus to come to the Earth and go to the cross. He accomplished
for us what we could not do for ourselves; reconciliation (making
us right) with God.

With all that said, I do believe *agape* love has an immediate and
developmental component. Close relationships do not have to be
present to reach out to others in meaningful ways. While working
on my Master of Arts in Christian Ministry, I virtually commuted
from Florida to Tennessee during a seven-year period. To help hold
down my costs, I often tried to stay with a Christian couple or in a
dorm while in Memphis. However, on this one particular occasion
it looked like I was out of luck. None of the places I typically stayed
at were available. Then, this gracious student, whom I had never
met, called me and asked if I would like to stay at his home. He
was going on a short trip, so I could have his home all to myself.
Then he suggested that I drive his truck rather than renting a car.
What a godsend! At one point, I had three in our family attending
universities at the same time, so money was tight. Somehow, he
was made aware of my situation and lovingly reached out to help
a Christian brother whom he had never met.

While our new caring orientation moves us to become involved
with others' needs, the life experiences gained from reaching out
to them also has a developmental impact on our hearts. We can
see how our expressions of love make a difference in the lives of
others. Such good works give the Holy Spirit fertile ground to aid
our transformation into the image of Christ. Our old uncaring, self-
seeking hearts begin to melt away and are replaced with compassionate, others-seeking hearts. When this occurs, responding
lovingly will become a natural extension of who we are, not something we have to be prompted to do. We now seek out opportunities to help others, like a hound dog on the trail of a fox.

My wife recently gave up her day off to go take care of a dear
friend who was recovering from surgery. Her unbegrudging de-

sire to do this kind deed was commendable, but what truly set it apart as special was her intentionality. Once she got the scent of a friend in need, she started to thoughtfully contemplate on ways she could more effectively help. The night before, she buzzed around the house preparing food and gathering various items to take with her to ease her friend's burden. Focused on her friend's needs, her love would not be demonstrated in a haphazard way. Reaching out in love to others signifies to the world whether you are one of God's own. Does your treatment of fellow Christians provide evidence to the world that you are a disciple of Christ?

Jesus and Benevolent Angels

Jesus encountered angels only twice during His ministry according to the four gospels. First during His temptation by Satan in the wilderness (Matthew 4:11; Mark 1:13), and second while praying in the Garden of Gethsemane (Luke 22:43). None of the gospels provide any details as to how the angels ministered to Jesus in the wilderness, but a few possibilities come to mind. Matthew and Luke mention that Jesus fasted for forty days, after which Satan tried to tempt Him in His weakened and hungry state (Matthew 4:2; Luke 4:2). Matthew mentioned that angels ministered to Jesus after Satan departed, so it seems very likely they would have provided Jesus sustenance, possibly similar to Elijah's experience.

Mark pointed out that the angels also ministered to Jesus throughout the forty days, while He was being tempted by Satan and among wild beasts (v. 13). Because Jesus' hunger played an important role in whether He would be tempted to turn the stones into bread, it seems unlikely that the angels provided Him sustenance during the forty days. Perhaps their ministry involved spiritual encouragement to stand up to Satan's temptations or to provide protection from the wild beasts, possibly akin to how the angel "shut the lions' mouths" while protecting Daniel in the lions' den (Daniel 6:22). Whatever the case, God recognized His Son's distress, and His concern for Jesus undoubtedly moved Him to send the ministering angels.

Turning to Jesus' second angelic encounter, we find Him in the Garden of Gethsemane. Facing horrific suffering, Jesus decided to retreat into the garden to pray to His Father (Mark 14:33-35). He took Peter, James and John with Him. Once separated from the other disciples, they noticed a sudden change in Jesus' demeanor. He previously exhibited the confident tone of a caring, master teacher, and abruptly He became visibly distressed and in deep anguish. Jesus stated, "My soul is deeply grieved to the point of death; remain here and keep watch" (v. 34). Jesus withdrew a little further from His beloved trio to gain a little solitude in which to talk to His Father. Luke provided us with a picture of our Savior's humanity as He went to God in prayer.

> How did a lone angel "shut" all those lions' mouths in the lions' den? Did he physically subdue their mouths and hold them back with his strength? Did he somehow curb the appetites of the beasts? Did he suppress their senses to Daniel's presence? Was Daniel made to be an unappetizing specimen? Whatever amazing power the angel possessed, won't it be interesting to have Daniel share the story with us some day?

> "Father, if You are willing, remove this cup from Me; yet not My will, but Yours be done." Now an angel from heaven appeared to Him, strengthening Him. And being in agony He was praying very fervently; and His sweat became like drops of blood, falling down upon the ground (Luke 22:42-44).

Jesus' extreme condition stirred His Father to send an angel to strengthen Him. But what was the "cup" that Jesus wanted removed? Some propose that the severity of Jesus' agony led Him to be concerned about prematurely dying thus being unable to fulfill His mission of going to the cross.[53] Perhaps the strengthening of the angel removed this "cup" (or concern). Jesus' statement that His soul was "deeply grieved, to the point of death" (Mark 14:34) would appear to support such a notion. However, "to the point of death" was a common Septuagint saying that expressed extremely deep sorrow.[54]

In Mark 10:32-34, Jesus shared with the apostles the destiny that awaited Him as they journeyed to Jerusalem together for the last time.

> Behold, we are going up to Jerusalem, and the Son of Man will be delivered to the chief priests and the scribes; and they will condemn Him to death, and will hand Him over to the Gentiles. They will mock Him and spit on Him, and scourge Him, and kill Him, and three days later He will rise again (vv. 33-34).

Immediately following this statement, James and John presumptuously requested to sit on Jesus' right and left hand upon His glorification. Disturbed by their continued lack of understanding, Jesus asked if they could "drink the cup that I drink" (v. 38). This obviously was a metaphor referring to His upcoming sufferings and death which He had just revealed to them. With the looming specter of the cross now before Jesus in the garden, it is reasonable to assume that Jesus continued to utilize this same metaphor.

A second more obvious reason for Jesus' severe agony was the excruciating painful death that awaited Him at the cross. In no uncertain terms, anticipation of such a death would terrify me to the core of my being. Last, the anticipation of becoming sin on our behalf (2 Corinthians 5:21) may have been a horrible burden to Jesus' holy nature.[55] Because sin possesses a separating quality from our holy God, it may have left Jesus alienated from His Father for the first time. With the answer not given directly to us, perhaps it was a combination of the last two options. The extreme stress from either of these would have left Jesus in a weakened state.

God's compassion for Jesus was demonstrated by sending an angelic comfort-giver, but what could a lone angel do to strengthen Jesus in the face of such a horrific trial? Conceivably, Jesus received physical strength through the touch of the angel, similar to how an angel imparted strength to weary Daniel: " 'As for me, there remains just now no strength in me, nor has any breath been left in me.' Then this one with the human appearance touched me again and strengthened me" (Daniel 10:17-18). Perhaps the angel was a sign that Jesus' prayer was heard (Hebrews 5:7), giving Him the confidence to press on, knowing God's will would be done.[56] The angel may also have represented the divine presence of His Father thus giving Jesus the spiritual encouragement He needed to resist temptation.[57] Possibly a simple message of encouragement from His Father or a gentle wiping of Jesus' brow helped bring Him through the crisis. The important thing to note was that God's attentive compassion for His Son's agony moved Him to reach out to Jesus.

We do not typically think of God's power being constrained, but His love for mankind and plan to redeem them curtailed His willingness to act in this situation. God's merciful heart must have sorely ached for His Son, knowing He had at His disposal the ability to end Jesus' suffering, but because mankind's salvation pivoted on the upcoming events, He would, like no other time in eternity, have to lean on His attribute of longsuffering.

I am sure many of you can recall the loving touch of your mother when you were sick as a child. Lifeless with a high fever, I remember my mother years ago gently stroking my face and chest with a wash cloth saturated with a water and alcohol solution. The cooling sensation of the treatment was wonderful, but what really mattered was the touch of my mother. Her presence and care brought extraordinary comfort. Knowing His Father was mindful of Him, must have brought renewed vigor to Jesus. For after receiving strength from the angel, Jesus was then prepared to face His betrayal and arrest. Resolute to endure undue horrors for the benefit of humankind, our Savior did what only He could do – go to the cross in our stead.

Questions

1. When Sarah used human reasoning to derive a scheme to provide Abraham with children through her maid Hagar, what were the results? How might she have handled this differently? How might this have changed the results?

2. Hagar was the first person in Scripture documented to have an angelic being sent to them. What does this teach us about God? What should we take from this story to affect our outreach to others today?

3. After Elijah's great victory over the prophets of Baal, would you have predicted his reaction to Jezebel's subsequent messenger? Explain your answer. How might Elijah have responded differently?

4. What were the physical and spiritual ramifications to what the angel did for Elijah? What does this teach us concerning how we should help others in times of distress?

5. Were you ever taken aback by the biblical command to love others? How has our culture potentially caused some confusion in regard to this command? What is the essence of the meaning of the biblical term *agape*?

6. How is love (*agape*) both developmental and immediate? Give some examples of both. What changes take place in Christians as the quality of love matures within them? How should Christians then respond in life to others? Do others perceive you as a loving person?

7. During His ministry, on what occasions did angels minister to Jesus? What are some possibilities of how they served Him? Why were the angels sent?

8. God's answer to Jesus' garden prayer was different than Jesus' direct request. God had the power to grant it, but what constrained Him? Do you think this may have been a troubling time for God? Pondering these things, what value does God place on His relationship to humankind?

9. Jesus chose to obey God's will and go to the cross; what other options might Jesus still have had at His disposal? Why did He not choose them? Is He not a wonderful Savior?

Chapter 7

Agents of
Answered Prayer

But the angel said to him, "Do not be afraid, Zacharias,
for your petition has been heard,
and your wife Elizabeth will bear you a son,
and you will give him the name John" (Luke 1:13).

On July 30, 1971, James Irwin worked diligently on deploying
the Central Station at the foot of the Moon's Apennine mountain
range. Keenly aware that this hardware served as the central hub
for several other scientific instruments, this Apollo 15 astronaut
knew that many scientists back on the earth depended on him to
successfully bring it on-line. Keeping to the procedure which was
integrated into the cuff of his spacesuit, Irwin was making good
progress until an unexpected malfunction occurred. Erecting hardware in a bulky spacesuit on the lunar surface was challenging
enough, but when combined with an unexpected anomaly, much
of the Apollo 15's scientific mission now faced failure. Because of
the time constraints, Irwin did not feel that consulting Houston
was an option, so he sought heavenly advice.[58] The following ex-
cerpt from Irwin's book, *To Rule the Night*, documents the result
of his prayer for help.

> ... I prayed. Immediately I had the answer. It was almost
> like a revelation. God was telling me what to do. ... I am

not talking about some vague sense of direction. There was this supernatural sensation of His presence. If I needed Him I could call on Him, call on His power.[59]

Irwin successfully deployed the Central Station and directly credits God's guidance. God's care and concern for him during the lunar surface phase of the mission had a profound effect on him and caused this privileged astronaut to deeply reflect on his purpose in life. He subsequently left NASA and became an evangelist. While we may not all have such obvious answers to our prayers, I believe most of us have reflected on situations in our lives and noted God's handiwork. He may not answer our prayers as we specifically fashion them; but with His greater purposes in mind, He nevertheless provides a response.

The fact that God listens to and answers our prayers is in itself a demonstration of His love for us. Giving others our attention and acting upon their requests shows that we care about them. Arriving home from work, many of you have surely experienced the joy of having one of your children run up to you eager to share his or her latest artwork. Often when we get in from work, all we really want to do is crash for a while. However, when our beloved child needs our attention, we set aside our desires and thoughtfully listen to his or her animated description and praise a wonderful masterpiece. Our steadfast interest along with seasoned responses may well serve to build the confidence crayon toting artists need to someday create the great artistic achievements of the future.

During the Sermon on the Mount, Jesus appealed to His disciples to seek God in prayer. To demonstrate how His Father lovingly responds to His children's requests, Jesus provided the following illustration:

> Or what man is there among you, when his son asks for a loaf, will give him a stone? Or if he asks for a fish, he will not give him a snake, will he? If you then, being evil, know how to give good gifts to your children, how much more

will your Father who is in heaven give what is good to those
who ask Him! (Matthew 7:9-11).

In our culture today, the question probably goes more like this,
"When his son shall ask him for a car, will you give him a unicycle?"
In every age, God loves us. He not only pays attention to us by listening to our requests but responds with good things (maybe not
always a new car though). Sometimes we may overlook the goodness in God's responses. However, He knows how to make it work
for good if we love Him (Romans 8:28).

We have already seen angels at work bringing God's responses
to the prayers of Jesus and Cornelius, but I would like to further highlight God's concern for the welfare of those He loves in the answers
to two more prayers. Most answers to prayer come with a quiet sub-
tleness, but in two interesting circumstances, Daniel and Peter had
angelic encounters that left no doubt to God's intentions.

Another Jailbreak

Years ago, I remember praying for the opportunity to study
God's Word with a friend and co-worker. This had been an ongoing prayer of mine, but for some reason I became much more
passionate about this request of God. As I recall, I petitioned God
the previous night, the following morning, and all the way into
work one hopeful day. I asked God to open a door of opportunity
so that I could approach my friend and give me the courage to
walk through it. (Of course if you're going to pray while driving,
please do it with your eyes open.) For me, praying while driving is
kind of like talking to a passenger. With the radio off and alone in
the car, I have found conversations with God to be very rich.
When I arrived at work that morning, I remember going into my
office and sitting down at my desk. Before becoming settled into
the day's routine, the young man I had been praying for came into
my office. Quietly, he shut the door, walked around my desk and
pulled up a chair right beside me. Knowing he had never done
this before, I silently exclaimed, "Lord, you've got to be kidding

me!" He proceeded to ask a question that I readily answered, and then the courage I prayed for came out; I asked him if he would like to study the Bible with me outside work hours. To this day his response still amazes me; he was overjoyed and felt truly honored that I would ask him to study with me. Oh how I wish that many of my other evangelistic outreach experiences had turned out like this one.

When he left my office, I sat there stunned. I could hardly believe what had just taken place. Did God intervene in our lives in so blatant a way or had this been only coincidence? He did have a question to ask me, but wow, this incident had God's fingerprints all over it! Over the next five years I studied on and off with him and his future wife. They both committed their lives to Christ, and I had the privilege of baptizing them. Since then, they have served God in various capacities and are raising three boys in the teachings of Christ. Today, I believe in no uncertain terms that God intervened in a mighty way in the circumstances involving their conversion. My prayers of passion were heard and answered. God taught me through this experience that He truly can "do far more abundantly beyond all that we ask or think, according to the power that works within us" (Ephesians 3:20).

Remarkable as my experience was, it pales in comparison to an incident Peter experienced. Even this Holy Spirit-inspired man was left "scratching his head" for a few minutes because of the surreal nature of his experience. The story unfolds in Acts 12 where we find King Herod Agrippa I actively persecuting Christians. During this period, he executed James, the apostle and the brother of John (v. 2). Discovering this increased his popularity with the Jews, Herod decided to garner a few more points with his countrymen by imprisoning Peter. Herod was gripped by a temptation that has probably troubled most of us from time to time; it is truly amazing what we will resort to in an effort to be pleasing in the eyes of others.

What devastating blows these turn of events must have been for the young Jerusalem church. Cries of anguish, desperation, and uncertainty most likely replaced these beleaguered Christians' psalms of joy. "How can this be happening?" "James, one of the Lord's closest apostles, is no longer with us." "And now Peter, our stalwart leader, is facing death." "What can we do against such a combination of hate and power?" "What can we do?"

Destitute, but they still had a highly effective tool – fervent prayer; "So Peter was kept in prison, but prayer for him was being made fervently by the church to God" (Acts 12:5). Fervent prayer is not for the timid. Marked by intensity, constancy, and often a flow of tears, fervent prayer cries out with a deep passion to the One who can come to our aid. Jesus in the Garden of Gethsemane, petitioned His Father "very fervently; and His sweat became like drops of blood, falling down upon the ground" (Luke 22:44). Most of us will face a time in our lives when we will need to resort to fervent prayer.

A number of years ago, just prior to Thanksgiving, I learned that my father was terminally ill with prostate cancer. My father and I were very close. Even when I was in my mid-thirties, my father hardly ever missed one of my softball games. Oh, how he would have loved being at my daughter's soccer games and my son's various sporting events. It was not to be.

Shortly after learning of my father's illness, I accompanied my wife to her appointment with an orthopedic surgeon. She broke her neck in a gymnastics accident in high school years earlier and was having some diagnostic procedures run because the level of pain she dealt with daily had become more intense. But neither of us was prepared for the upcoming news. When the doctor came in the room, he was noticeably agitated. While viewing her MRIs, he mumbled that he did not know how my wife survived such a traumatic accident. He went on to tell us that he believed there was a terminal process going on with my wife's spinal cord. With my dad already facing death, this additional news took me into a deep pit of despair.

We drove to a secluded spot and sat and held each other for the longest time with tears flowing uncontrollably. A haunting thought plagued me during this time; "Would my children lose their mother at such a young age? Being a father is overwhelming enough but to take on the role of a mom as well; heaven help me." As you might imagine, I became acquainted with fervent prayer. Our prayers would be joyfully answered about a month later, when we learned from a cervical spine specialist that he did not believe my wife's condition was terminal. His diagnosis turned out to be correct. Life's unexpected twists and turns can confront us with some devastating circumstances. But we know for certain that we have a loving God who attentively hears the fervent requests of His people.

> A squad consisted of four soldiers, so there were sixteen soldiers assigned to guard Peter. Four squads allowed the solders to rotate and stay fresh through the night watch.[60]

As the church fervently prayed for Peter, four squads of soldiers vigilantly guarded over him (Acts 12:4). The night before Herod planned on making a spectacle of Peter before the Jews, God decided to act – another jailbreak was in order (see the story of the Acts 5 jailbreak in Chapter 5). His people needed a shot in the arm, so God intervened in an impressive fashion.

... Peter was sleeping between two soldiers, bound with two chains, and guards in front of the door were watching over the prison. And behold, an angel of the Lord suddenly appeared and a light shone in the cell; and he struck Peter's side and woke him up saying, "Get up quickly." And his chains fell off his hands. And the angel said to him, "Gird yourself and put on your sandals." And he did so. And he said to him, "Wrap your cloak around you and follow me." And he went out and continued to follow, and he did not know that what was being done by the angel was real, but thought he was seeing a vision. When they had passed the first and second guard, they came to the iron gate that leads into the city, which opened for them by itself; and they went out and went along one street, and immediately the angel departed from him (Acts 12:6-10).

What a spectacular array of the supernatural! An angel appeared out of nowhere, the prison cell was suddenly illuminated, and Peter's chains miraculously fell off his hands. The guards on each side of Peter were totally unaware of the escape in progress; Peter and the angel passed by two other guards undetected, and the prison gate mysteriously opened by itself. So bizarre were the circumstances associated with the jailbreak that Peter could not even believe his eyes; he thought the whole episode was a vision.

God loved Peter, but He rescued him because of the church's fervent prayers. That was why Luke noted it in the account. Not only did God save Peter, but He showed a struggling group of Christians that He was still in control and cared for them. God wants us to pray. All of our prayers need not be fervent in nature. Some prayers may take on a serious tone; others may take on a joyful one. But we must ask ourselves this question: "Have I been giving God the opportunity to show His concern for me and others through my prayers?"

Indifference is one of the most insidious character issues within God's people. It is not that we don't care; we just don't care enough to bring about action. Our own selfish desires and concerns consume our thoughts and even pervert our prayer life. I remember one Sunday morning when an individual came forward during the invitation and tearfully requested prayers of the congregation. A week later at my small group meeting, I asked if anyone had been praying for this heartbroken individual. I received a bunch of blank stares. I appreciated the truth, but they understood their neglect. These were good people, but there was no *agape*. The lack of *agape* in a church will make it dysfunctional and heartless. I would suggest that you jot down the prayer requests of others. Review them for a moment before you start to pray and make these requests to God before the ones concerning yourself. God loves others; do we? What you pray about will give you the answer.

A Harbinger of Hope

Daniel 9 opens with the book's loyal prophet digging into Scripture. Daniel found in Jeremiah's writings that the "desolations of Jerusalem" were to be complete in seventy years (v. 2). Knowing the time must be at hand, he prayed for God to press on with the restoration of the holy city and His people, who had been in exile in Babylon for what must have seemed like an eternity. Before looking at this passage for our intended purpose, I would like to take a brief aside and point out a few noteworthy items.

First, as Daniel deliberated over God's Word, he obviously reflected on the gravity of it to himself and God's people. When reading the Bible, we too often treat it as an intellectual exercise. Bible knowledge is important, but our readings should also be a place where we spiritually "encounter" God. As the writer of Hebrews said, we need to allow God's Word to be "living and active," piercing all the way to the "soul and spirit," and judging "the thoughts and intentions of the heart" (Hebrews 4:12). God demands that we change; we are to become like His Son. God's Word should be allowed to probe the depths of who we are and find points of departure from Christ.[61] Our readings may also lead us to the realization that our controlling nature has steered us away from God's purpose for us. In either case, we now have something to truly pray about.

How Daniel approached God in prayer also serves as an excellent example for us today. Daniel was seeking forgiveness for himself and the nation of Israel. Prior to coming before God on this matter, Daniel prepared himself by fasting, along with wearing sackcloth and sitting in ashes (Daniel 9:3). His fasting demonstrated his devotion to God, and the serious nature of the matter he was bringing before Him. The sackcloth and ashes indicated Daniel's mourning of the sins being confessed as well as showing humility. Kind of makes our bedtime prayers look rather wimpy.

These attitudes that Daniel exhibited when he approached God, should also flood our hearts today whenever we come before Him seeking mercy for our actions. Forgiveness for our sins is a serious matter. The expense paid by God was unfathomable. So when we come before the God of grace for forgiveness, we should prostrate ourselves before Him and make our request known in a truly sorrowful and faithful manner.

We can definitely learn from how Daniel humbled himself as he confessed His nation's rebellion, but I find how he honored God in his prayer to be truly inspirational (Daniel 9:4-19). I know we hold God in high regard but do we express it in our prayers? To Daniel, God is great, awesome, trustworthy (keeps His covenant), loving, righteous, compassionate, forgiving, and mighty. And it was only for his glorious God's namesake that his prayer should be answered.

> ... for we are not presenting our supplications before You on account of any merits of our own, but on account of Your great compassion. O Lord, hear! O Lord, forgive! O Lord, listen and take action! For Your own sake, O my God, do not delay, because Your city and Your people are called by Your name (vv. 18-19).

Not only was the removal of punishment at stake, God's name had been shamed.

As children of God, our open sin and rebellion against Him bring reproach on His name. Daniel's prayer brings to light this failing, along with the proper response. We should desire the cleansing power of Christ's blood to purify us and the chance to lead faithful, holy lives to bring honor to God's name.

Bringing us back to the purpose of the book, I want to call attention to another item from the above text. Daniel appealed to God to act in harmony with one of His fundamental character traits – "great compassion."[62] And God wasted no time in compassionately reaching out to His distraught prophet.

Now while I was speaking and praying, and confessing my sin and the sin of my people Israel, and presenting my supplication before the LORD my God in behalf of the holy mountain of my God, while I was still speaking in prayer, then the man Gabriel, whom I had seen in the vision previously, came to me in my extreme weariness about the time of the evening offering. He gave me instruction and talked with me and said, "O Daniel, I have now come forth to give you insight with understanding. At the beginning of your supplications the command was issued, and I have come to tell you, for you are highly esteemed; so give heed to the message and gain understanding of the vision" (Daniel 9:20-23).

> The phrase translated "in my extreme weariness" (NASB) that applies to Daniel in Daniel 9:21 has been translated by others as "in swift flight" (e.g. NIV) and would apply to Gabriel. Obviously, such a rendering would support that angels had wings. I believe this translation is unlikely for several reasons. First, the text refers to Gabriel as a "man." Wings are not typical equipment of most men, so one would expect the author to have noted wings if they were actually present. Second, because Daniel had been fasting, the "in my extreme weariness" would seem to be a superior fit. Daniel also experienced weariness in the presence of other angels (see Daniel 10:8-9). Third, Stephen R. Miller points out that the Hebrew is lacking a conjectural verb that is necessary to support "in swift flight."[63]

Now that's an answer to a prayer! Before you can rise from your knees, an angel appears by your side to reveal God's reply.

God's love for Daniel became apparent in several ways through sending Gabriel with a divine message. First, by sending the great herald Gabriel with an immediate answer to Daniel's prayer, God confirmed in Daniel's heart that He truly was a God of great compassion. Presence is golden, and Gabriel represented the Almighty. When we take the time to be present during the special events of others or in their times of need, it shows that we care for them and provides an opportunity to pass on uplifting words. Attending special events of our youth can be extremely effective in creating an ongoing dialogue with them. By going to their soccer games or music recitals, they will realize that you care about them and in the future these events can serve as a common experience to develop a deeper relationship.

God also passed on words of endearment to Daniel. During his introduction, Gabriel described Daniel's standing with the Lord; "for you are highly esteemed." The New King James and New Revised Standard Versions translate the Hebrew term for "highly esteemed" as "greatly beloved." It carries the connotation that Daniel was precious and highly valued in God's eyes.[64] Early in my NASA career, I became close friends with my first boss. I remember asking him one day if I could be included in a particular activity, and he said, "Of course; you're family." To be viewed by him in that manner has always meant a great deal to me. Warm words of affection go a long way in building committed relationships. Can you imagine the size of the goose bumps that must have popped up on Daniel when he learned of God's feelings for him? He loves us too.

Last, Gabriel's message brought hope to the lamenting prophet. God, though cryptically, reveals His plan for the restoration of Israel and the coming Messiah (Daniel 9:24-27). Sometimes we just need hope to keep us going, and that is what God gave Daniel through Gabriel's message. The message revealed that Daniel's people would not remain in Babylon forever, and Jerusalem would not remain desolated. Hope of returning home and rebuilding the great city of David would reinvigorate the careworn, enslaved Jews.

As I started my junior year in high school, playing baseball was the only sport on my radar screen. However, once basketball season rolled around, I realized I had a shot at making the team. Because my school had just opened, the seniors in our district were given an option to remain at the school they had been attending or come to the new school. Not surprisingly, all the returning basketball seniors stayed loyal to their long-standing coach and remained at the other school in town. Because the coach at my new school was hurting for basketball talent, I decided to give it a try. Not much height and our inexperience appeared to be a recipe for disaster for our fledgling team, and the initial scores of our games seemed to validate the recipe. After being clobbered by about 50 to 60 points in some of our opening games, the situation looked hopeless.

As you might imagine, being shellacked game after game was tough for a bunch of emotionally-challenged teenage boys. Yet, our coach hung in there with us. He knew the game of basketball and had a knack for teaching its fundamentals. He saw to it that we were in top-notch shape, and we spent an inordinate amount of time executing drills to sharpen our skills. On top of all that, he made it fun and obviously believed in us. He turned us into basketball players and teammates. We went 0-25, but by the end of the season our margin of defeat was down to only three points. Our coach had instilled *hope* in us, and by experiencing such a radical improvement, we new better times were on the horizon.

When the next season rolled around, we won our first game early on. As the game clock went to all zeros, an overwhelming sense of relief rushed over us, followed quickly by a crazed euphoria. We broke a horrible streak, and it felt like the world had been lifted from our shoulders. We went on to post a record of 8-18, which sounds bad, but an 8 game improvement from one season to the next is a significant achievement. Even with the 0-25 season, I would gladly relive that life situation. Energized by a hope of what we could become, our coach empowered us to overcome our humble beginnings.

Hope allows us to carry on when life throws us a curve. The writer of Hebrews describes the Christian's hope "as an anchor of the soul" (Hebrews 6:19). Hope in God's promises in Christ Jesus keeps us stable as the currents of the world try to set us adrift. God's promises allow us to project a brighter future, and hope in their realization serves as a powerful motivator. God's gospel provides the hope of forgiveness, liberation, change, and eternal life; and this hope is firmly anchored to the immovable Rock.

God knew Daniel needed hope that originated from Him. The years of exile away from Jerusalem had taken its toll on Daniel and his people, and some form of hope from God was sorely needed. A visit from Gabriel along with God's personal message of reassurance was just what Daniel needed.

As God prepared Gabriel to be a harbinger of hope to Daniel, He has also equipped us to be messengers of hope to others – a hope that is firmly anchored in His truth and Christ Jesus. My wife and I have noted incidents in our lives when we felt compelled to visit or call certain people. God used us to help them through some rough times and give them hope. The "hope" the world offered them had knocked them for a loop. They needed us to show them the way out of chaos by introducing some of God's principles for living while being empathetic to their situations. God was at work in these circumstances, and He expected us to do our part. It was God's initiative to send Gabriel to Daniel. Perhaps He is trying to send you to someone in need today; you may be His privileged harbinger of hope.

Questions

1. How can we surmise that God loves us because He listens and answers our prayers? Understanding our cultural sensitivities, how might we become confused about God's feelings for us based on His answers to our prayers? How might an answer contrary to our desires still show love?

2. Why did God send an angel to free Peter from prison? What was the condition of the Jerusalem church upon Peter's imprisonment? Looking at the big picture, what was the result of God freeing Peter?

3. Have you ever experienced a situation in life where you had no control over the outcome? How did it make you feel? What is an effective tool during such situations?

4. Why is indifference a detriment to our Christian walk? How might indifference work its way into our prayer life? What are some ways to remove indifference from our dealings with others?

5. What are some positive attributes to how Daniel approached God in prayer in Daniel 9? Is his approach applicable today? If so, how can you work such attributes into your prayers?

6. How did God answer Daniel's prayer? How was it an expression of love?

7. Why is hope important to our Christian walk? How has God equipped us to be messengers of hope? Can you identify someone today that you can serve by providing them with a message of hope?

Part 5

Justice of God

Justice Prelude

Have you ever yearned for someone just to follow through on what they said they would do? Over the years, even some of my closest friends and co-workers have let me down in this regard. When it becomes apparent late in the game that someone neglected to take care of an assigned responsibility, stress levels unavoidably go up, and tremendous energy will usually be required to overcome their irresponsibility. We often longingly desire for the proverbial "someone" who is "as good as their word" to come to our aid. God *is* that someone. His laws, words and actions are a natural expression of who He is. We actually could say that God is "as perfect as His word." In a comprehensive fashion, the psalmist portrays the wonderfully ideal quality of God's laws and declarations; His laws are perfect, testimonies sure, precepts right, commandment pure, and judgments true and righteous (Psalm 19:7-9).

Every action that proceeds from God is consistent with His perfect nature and laws; this is referred to as His righteousness.[65] Because God demonstrates righteousness by conducting Himself in a manner consistent with His laws, He wants His people to conform to these same standards which produce righteous living. God's righteous requirements have not only been conveyed through written commandments but became fully revealed to us in the life of Christ Jesus (John 1:14-18). And under the new covenant, God aids His people by writing His laws upon our hearts and minds (Hebrews 10:16; 2 Corinthians 3:3). We consequently live in a moral kingdom that God administers by a set of perfect standards (or laws) that has been delivered to us, and His judgments are always based on these same standards; we aptly refer to this as God's justice. Living in a kingdom ruled by the principles of righteousness and justice compelled the psalmist to praise its exalted Ruler; "The LORD reigns, let the earth rejoice; ... Righteousness and justice are the foundation of His throne" (Psalm 97:1-2). Have you ever praised God for His just approach to dealing with us?

Woven into the fabric of God's justice is His impartiality. He will apply the same standard to all of us. I have undertaken the dilemma of treating others equally, but I have found that this is not always easy. Our learned preferences and self-serving desires lurk in the background of our minds and cause undue sway on our judgments. I remember coaching girl's youth soccer with a friend who had a short list of rules that he wanted the girls to live by, such as not skipping practices, arriving at games thirty minutes early, and so forth. He impartially stuck to the rules no matter who you were. It did not matter if you were destined for a scholarship or the team's weakest link; you were treated equally, even if it meant the team might lose a game because the team's star would not be allowed to play. Through tirades by *prima donna* athletes and the wrath of poorly principled parents, he weathered many storms, yet remained true to his rules and treated all equally. With the perverted importance our society places on winning, the practice of good ethics is often discarded. What a breath of fresh air it was to witness such an honorable approach to treating others impartially.

At times, Scripture may appear to present God as being partial to the poor, but a closer examination reveals otherwise. Because the life circumstances of the poor make them vulnerable to unjust oppression, God's Word includes many warnings concerning their fair treatment.[66] However, God's direction to the judges demonstrates His impartial approach to administering justice: "You shall do no injustice in judgment; you shall not be partial to the poor nor defer to the great, but you are to judge your neighbor fairly" (Leviticus 19:15).[67] Moses proclaims that God is an "awesome God who does not show partiality nor take a bribe" (Deuteronomy 10:17). In the context of the judgment, Paul declares, "[T]here is no partiality with God" (Romans 2:11). Peter also claims that God is "the One who impartially judges according to each one's work" (1 Peter 1:17). Scripture is clear, God does not show favoritism; each will be judged impartially by his actions against the same standard.

We can see in God's Word that His justice entails the distribution of rewards to the righteous and the punishment of the wicked. Before going into Canaan, Moses taught the Israelites of the blessings that come from keeping God's commandments and the dire consequences to be faced by those who oppose Him.

> Know therefore that the LORD your God, He is God, the faithful God, who keeps his covenant and his lovingkindness to a thousandth generation with those who love him and keep his commandments; but repays those who hate him to their faces, to destroy them; .... Therefore, you shall keep the commandment and the statutes and the judgments which I am commanding you today, to do them (Deuteronomy 7:9-11).

Under the New Covenant, Paul communicated to the church in Rome that this same theme will continue to be followed by God.

> But because of your stubbornness and unrepentant heart you are storing up wrath for yourself in the day of wrath and revelation of the righteous judgment of God, who WILL RENDER TO EACH PERSON ACCORDING TO HIS DEEDS: to those who by perseverance in doing good seek for glory and honor and immortality, eternal life; but to those who are selfishly ambitious and do not obey the truth, but obey unrighteousness, wrath and indignation (Romans 2:5-8).

Whether we are rich or poor, royalty or laborer, famous or unknown, God will treat all equitably as He will render to both the righteous and the wicked their due.

God's justice does not only come into play at the Final Judgment, but Scripture informs us that His judgments have been cast throughout the history of the world.[68] This includes judgments of cataclysmic proportions as well as lesser events throughout the ages, such as the banishment of humankind from the garden of Eden, the flood, the destruction of Sodom and Gomorrah, the replacement of King Saul with David, the exile of Judah into Babylonian captivity, and the death of Herod Agrippa I. Nevertheless, during this life it often appears that unrighteous people gain from their sinful ways and escape punishment. To compound this perceived injustice, they seem to live comfortable lives with much wealth and many of life's luxuries. We relate to the psalmist's bewildered heart as he pondered the prosperity of the wicked; "And always at ease, they have increased in wealth. Surely in vain I have kept my heart pure ... " (Psalm 73:12-13). At times, it just does not seem fair. This is where our world of quick fixes plays tricks on us. Our culture trains us to focus on the here and now. God's justice addresses the eternal, and His justice will not be complete until the life beyond.[69] With our finite view and limited understanding, God could be perceived as unjust if we evaluate His justice on a short-term basis. It is important to realize the eternal nature of God's divine plan, and His justice will be vindicated at the end-time for eternity.[70]

In the next two chapters, we will see that God makes extensive use of His angels as He judiciously governs His creation. These stories will cast some light on areas we often keep dim. Angels frequently play a role in God's judgments that is not congruent with our culture's conception of these ominous beings, and we would much prefer to reflect on a God of grace than one of judgment. To truly understand the God of the Bible, His attribute of justice must be harmoniously integrated into our concept of Him. It is to the Scripture's stories of heavenly justice that we now turn to seek this knowledge and understanding.

Chapter 8

The Divine Council

*whereas angels who are greater in might and power
do not bring a reviling judgment against them
before the Lord (2 Peter 2:11).*

Brooks Robinson, the iconic third baseman of the Baltimore Orioles, profoundly impacted my youthful passions. A poster of this gifted Hall of Famer hung above my bed in my youth. Daily, my hero summoned me to an ever-increasing love of baseball. Aspiring to be like him, baseball bats and gloves carried far more value to me than any old toy. Excitement always gripped me as baseball season drew near. Rubbing down my glove with neats-foot oil to soften the leather was like sharpening a sword for battle. A soft, pliable glove helped you spear and hang on to the opposition's screaming line drives. But nothing held more joy for me than breaking out my collection of bats. To ready myself for the season, I remember practicing my swing in front of the mirror in our living room (forgive me Mom). I also would strip our palm trees of these really hard berries and hit them into the woods while playing a make-believe game. In my neighborhood, we played whatever sport was in season, and when baseball came around we played it with a tennis ball in a court at the end of a street. We painted the bases on the asphalt and had designated markers for home runs; what great fun!

Once Little League practice started, the fun really began. Practices were almost as enjoyable as games; especially batting practice. I craved the feeling of hitting a baseball on the "sweet spot" of the bat, driving it deep over the outfielders' heads. The excitement culminated once opening day rolled around. Sporting our cool uniforms, all the teams were introduced, pictures were taken, and then we had a huge picnic. One of my most memorable moments came on an opening day, when I was twelve years old. Our team was privileged to open the season with the first game. A pretty good-sized crowd hung around to watch our game to finish off the day's festivities. On my first at bat, I hit a home run over the center field fence, landing right in the middle of a parked car's roof. Among my twelve-year-old peers, I was a hero. Not only had I hit the first home run of the season, but I dented a car's roof in the process. As this season came to a close, I led my team in home runs, triples, singles, runs batted in, and batting average. Primed and ready for the all-star team, this particular summer promised to be a fun one; at least that's what I thought. After the last game, my coach pulled me aside and informed me that I had not been selected for the all-star team, but four of my teammates had. As I remember it, one was the league president's son, one was the head umpire's son, and two were coach's kids. My coach and father were livid about the situation, but nothing changed. At twelve years old, I only felt hurt. Several years would have to pass before I understood what truly transpired. I experienced my first tough lesson that life is not always fair.

Committees, councils, and various other types of decision-making bodies will always be burdened with biases and agendas. Each member brings his or her own predispositions into the mix. Their unique life experiences have formed who they are and will hold significant influence on how they view certain situations and people. Often these serve as strengths, but they can also adversely affect a group. These biases may be unconscious and hard to remove from the decision-making process. Hopefully, others can open our eyes to these unjust predispositions if they are detrimental. On the other hand, I have also encountered my fair share of individuals who are well aware of their biases and hold fast to self-serving agendas. I have experienced this in all walks of life; whether serving on committees at NASA or church, or while helping out with youth sports. Some people go to great extremes to manipulate a group to go along with their preferred course of action. I have witnessed and experienced subtle maneuvers, bold onslaughts, and demeaning attacks by others as they tried to control a group's decision. In general, I think the use of a well-chartered committee is wise, but the bottom line is that flawed decisions from groups are bound to happen. We can do our best to neutralize destructive prejudices and agendas; but we live in a corrupted world, and at times "unfair" will happen.

But what of heaven's decisions? Are they going to be fair? Our hopes and promises are grounded in a God who is perfectly just, so some reassurance along these lines should reinforce our faith. Angels appear throughout the Bible engaged in God's judicial administration. I hope to integrate this information for you in the coming pages in an attempt to draw conclusions concerning God's attribute of justice. I have never heard a sermon, lecture, or participated in a Sunday school class on this topic; so this will likely be new information for you. With all the injustice we have witnessed and experienced in this world, our hearts long for fairness that is pure and evenhanded for all.

Council of the Angels

Throughout the Old Testament, we find a veiled concept presented that God has a council of heavenly hosts. Many scholars refer to this as the divine council (or court). God's Word does not provide a systematic explanation for this august assembly, but several fleeting looks into its existence and function will prove helpful in understanding God's just nature. In Psalm 89:5-7, the psalmist declared that the angels may be mighty, but their meager powers hold no comparison to God's. For this reason, the "council of the holy ones" should praise and revere their Lord.

The heavens will praise Your wonders, O LORD; Your faithfulness also in the assembly of the holy ones. For who in the skies is comparable to the LORD? Who among the sons of the mighty is like the LORD, A God greatly feared in the council of the holy ones, And awesome above all those who are around Him? O LORD God of hosts, who is like You, O mighty LORD? (vv. 5-8a).

Because of the Psalms' poetic character, we must ask if this image of a council of angelic beings provides an actual view into the heavenly realm or was it poetic artistry to convey God's majesty. If it is a genuine portrayal, what are the roles and responsibilities of the council and its members?

Before proceeding on to some additional helpful passages, an important observation lays before us. Many of us struggle with humility. We tend to think that we are a little more important than we actually are. When angels revere God, they develop humility. They recognize that His awesome power far exceeds their own. This acquired posture of humility then enables them to genuinely praise God. I have found it hard to praise another from a prideful heart. Let us learn from our heavenly counterparts and push aside our pride and revere God. Only He is truly praiseworthy. Solomon's advice ring's forever true; "The fear of the LORD is the beginning of wisdom" (Proverbs 9:10).

> The Hebrew term translated as "council" in Psalm 89:7 carries with it the connotation of the "counsel" that is also given. This suggests that "the council of the holy ones" may be an advice-giving body.[71]

An Appointed Day

The Book of Job describes two events that potentially offer a glimpse into the divine council.

> Now there was a day when the sons of God came to present themselves before the LORD, and Satan also came among them (Job 1:6).

> Again there was a day when the sons of God came to present themselves before the LORD, and Satan also came among them to present himself before the LORD (2:1).

These verses are fairly vague, so can we truly deduce from them that a formal assembly took place? An organized gathering appears to be implied for several reasons. Because the occasion was repeated, it lends credence to the belief that the assemblies occurred regularly.[72] The designation "there was a day" gives the connotation that these gatherings occurred on an appointed day.[73] The phrase "present themselves" literally means that the sons of God "stationed themselves" as royal attendants before their King.[74] A plurality of divine beings assembled on the same occasion also suggests this was a formal gathering. This reminds me somewhat of the center director's staff meetings at KSC. They were regularly scheduled meetings, when he gathered together his senior management team. He utilized these formal meetings to pass on crucial information, make assignments, and listen to his staff's reports. When important decisions needed to be entertained, special council meetings would also be convened.

In both these instances in Job, God used these opportunities to query Satan about his whereabouts and his thoughts on Job. However, the author included no dialogue between God and any of the angels, but such conversations were probably not relevant to the story of Job and thus not included. These passages potentially point to a formal time when God meets with some of His heavenly subjects, but more substantive Scripture will be needed for us to draw any reasonable conclusions.

Daniel's Interpretation and Vision

The Book of Daniel contributes two additional occasions that offer further insight into the potential existence of a divine council. The first involved Daniel's interpretation of a dream, while the second concerned a vision Daniel himself beheld. During the Babylonian captivity of the Jews, King Nebuchadnezzar of Babylon had a disturbing dream of a great tree and its demise (Daniel 4). Uneasy as to its meaning, he sought an interpretation from Babylon's so-called wise men – diviners, magicians, and the like. Once they failed to make sense of the dream, Daniel came to the King's aid. Nebuchadnezzar explained that he beheld a vision of a beautiful and immense tree; visible throughout the entire earth. This wonderful tree provided a dwelling place and sustenance for the living creatures of the earth. While he pondered this vision, an alarming incident occurred; "an angelic watcher, a holy one, descended from heaven" (v. 13) and delivered the following message:

> Chop down the tree and cut off its branches, Strip off its foliage and scatter its fruit; Let the beasts flee from under it And the birds from its branches. Yet leave the stump with its roots in the ground, But with a band of iron and bronze around it In the new grass of the field; And let him be drenched with the dew of heaven, And let him share with the beasts in the grass of the earth. Let his mind be changed from that of a man And let a beast's mind be given to him, And let seven periods of time pass over him. This sentence is by the decree of the angelic watchers And the decision is a command of the holy ones, In order that the living may know That the Most High is ruler over the realm of mankind, And bestows it on whom He wishes, And sets over it the lowliest of men (Daniel 4:14-17).

After a night of strange dreams, I have often asked myself, "Where did that come from?" Besides thinking I may be a bit weird, I readily forget the dreams and carry on with my day's activities. Nebuchadnezzar though, was haunted by the superstitions of his day, so such a dream left him frightened of what might await him. And frightened he should have been, because this dream was a dire warning from Israel's mighty God.

> Due to nuances in the Hebrew language, it could be argued that the watcher only delivered the ruling on behalf of God. This is the New International Version's translation approach. However, when viewed in conjunction with the court room vision of Daniel 7, which we will review in a moment, I am inclined to believe that we have been given the results of a deliberation and judgment of the divine council.

The language of Daniel 4:17 appears to support that the angels participated in deriving a verdict, though Daniel points out that the ultimate decision was God's (v. 24). The two parallel phrases "This sentence is by the decree of the angelic watchers" and "the decision is a command of the holy ones" (v. 17) serve to emphasize the serious nature of the verdict. The holy ones of heaven had heartily joined God in determining a suitable judgment against the great tree. From their perspective, the great tree's demeanor was an affront against God's sovereign rule, and their decree leaves no confusion of who should be recognized as the "Most High" ruler (v. 17). In the following verses, Daniel revealed that Nebuchadnezzar was the great tree. Until Nebuchadnezzar recognized that "Heaven" ruled (v. 26), his kingdom would be taken from him. However, the merciful Judge let the prophecy serve as a warning for twelve months to see if the haughty king would repent.

Nebuchadnezzar's accomplishments blurred his ability to recognize God's role in his life. Sound a little familiar? I think we've all been there. His achievements fed a prideful character that elevated his self-importance. Because he did not heed the warnings of the prophecy but continued to celebrate his glory rather than

God's (Daniel 4:30), Nebuchadnezzar's fate became a degrading one. He joined the beasts of the field and ate grass for seven years. Kind of makes some of our trials seem a bit trite, doesn't it?

Unlike Nebuchadnezzar, the angels eagerly humble themselves and choose to glorify God. Let's follow our heavenly counterparts' lead and remove the words of pride from our vocabulary, before we find ourselves enjoying a little hay *du jour* (metaphorically speaking of course). From one of the most humiliating life experiences ever encountered, Nebuchadnezzar came to his senses and left us with the following words concerning God; "Now I, Nebuchadnezzar, praise, exalt and honor the King of heaven, for all His works are true and His ways just, and He is able to humble those who walk in pride" (Daniel 4:37). Are such words easy for you to express?

At a later date, Daniel begins to remove a little more haze from our cloudy picture of the divine council. During his vision of the four beasts in Daniel 7, Daniel saw a dramatic display of God's divine court coming to session.

> I kept looking Until thrones were set up, and the Ancient of Days took His seat; His vesture was like white snow And the hair of His head like pure wool His throne was ablaze with flames, Its wheels were a burning fire. A river of fire was flowing And coming out from before Him; Thousands upon thousands were attending Him, And myriads upon myriads were standing before Him; The court sat, And the books were opened (Daniel 7:9-10).

The court then proceeded to pass judgment on the four beasts, which represent four kingdoms (vv. 11-12). What an awesome scene of God's majesty!

What in this narrative leads us to believe that angelic beings played an active role in this court scene? In Daniel 7:9, "thrones" were being set up, not just God's throne. After God took a seat, the rest of "the court" sat (v. 10), undoubtedly in the thrones set

up for them. In verse 26, Daniel again referred to the court con-
vening to cast a judgment. Daniel did not tell us who sat on the
thrones or what specifically was their function. However, having
thrones to sit upon in the presence of Almighty God lends credence to these beings' importance. Perhaps these members of
the heavenly court were the twenty-four elders of John's revelatory vision that sat on the twenty-four thrones that surrounded
God's throne (Revelation 4:4). Also, the title of "the court" served
to separate them in importance from the other thousands that attended to God. From all this, I believe we can reasonably assume
that the court was somehow involved in the judicial process, that
is God did not act unilaterally. Although, God retained the ultimate responsibility for passing the final judgments, and because
His rulings were in favor of the saints, the vision clearly portrayed
Him as a righteous Judge (Daniel 7:22, 27).

Micaiah's Enticing Vision

The prophet Micaiah's vision of the throne room of God adds
a little more clarity to the divine council's activity, but Scripture
does not fine tune this picture any further. The vision was precipitated by King Ahab's desire to take back Ramoth-gilead from the
Syrians (1 Kings 22:1-23). He solicited Jehoshaphat, king of Judah,
to join Israel in this cause. Jehoshaphat agreed but requested
Ahab consult God on the matter. Ahab paraded in four hundred
supposed prophets, who readily supported his desire for battle,
but Jehoshaphat detected that the allegiance of these "prophets"
rendered their predictions useless and asked, "Is there not yet a
prophet of the LORD here that we may inquire of him?" (v. 7).

While at NASA, I remember dealing with a couple of contractor employees whose allegiance was to their company, not to
NASA's greater mission. This often tainted what they told me. After
arriving at this understanding, I sought the information I needed
from other sources. Ahab's four hundred prophets were not
aligned with God's purposes, so Jehoshaphat knew they could not
be trusted. Ahab reluctantly sent for the prophet Micaiah, but he

detested him because Micaiah prophesied contrary to Ahab's self-serving will. Micaiah's subsequent prophecy surprisingly agreed with the other prophets. In another shocking turn, Ahab scolded Micaiah for agreeing with them; "How many times must I adjure you to speak to me nothing but the truth in the name of the LORD?" (1 Kings 22:16). Micaiah then shared a vision predicting Ahab's defeat. With Ahab still disgruntled, Micaiah reinforced the serious nature of his prophecy by sharing a second vision.

> Therefore hear the word of the LORD. I saw the LORD sitting on His throne, and all the host of heaven standing by Him on His right and on His left. The LORD said, "Who will entice Ahab to go up and fall at Ramoth-gilead?" And one said this while another said that. Then a spirit came forward and stood before the LORD and said, "I will entice him." The LORD said to him, "How?" And he said, "I will go out and be a deceiving spirit in the mouth of all the prophets." Then He said, "You are to entice him and also prevail. Go and do so." Now therefore, behold, the LORD has put a deceiving spirit in the mouth of all these your prophets; and the LORD has proclaimed disaster against you (vv. 19-23).

What a fascinating vision. With such privileged insight, we can easily understand Micaiah's desire to promote only God's word and not himself; "As the LORD lives, what the LORD says to me, that I shall speak" (v. 14). God gives us this same glimpse through His Word; how does it serve to impact our faith today?

Several important observations can be made from Micaiah's vision. He appeared to join the divine council already in progress. God was already seated on His throne with the heavenly hosts in attendance. A judgment concerning Ahab had been made earlier; he was to "fall at Ramoth-gilead." But intriguingly, God requested input on how His judgment should be carried out. Micaiah observed the angels debating over this; "And one said this while another said that" (1 Kings 22:20). Finally, a spirit brought God an acceptable solution and was commissioned to carry out the plan. Is it not interesting that the omniscient God of the universe included the angels in the deliberation of how His judgment would be implemented?

As a backdrop to our current story, God had already judged Ahab for the murder of Naboth in 1 Kings 21. After Elijah told the king of the devastating sentence upon him and his household (vv.17-24), Ahab humbled himself before the Lord (vv. 27-29). God decided to delay part of the judgment, but Ahab's death sentence would still come to pass. Whether God included the angels in this initial deliberation phase of Ahab's judgment, we were not told. However, another insightful aspect of God's justice calls out to us from these narratives. Even though God's judgment against Ahab had been determined, God continued to reach out to Ahab. Two visions warned the king of his demise. Sharing the vision of the divine council's conclusion was an extraordinary attempt by God to engage Ahab.[75] Yet the king's obstinate self-will stood in stark opposition to God's will, and Ahab's egotistical heart could not muster any humility this time. Ahab's execution took place on the battlefield through a bowshot of the enemy. Ahab's legacy was one of unparalleled evil among Israel's kings; while God stood just and fair for his actions in the eyes of His people.

What Are We to Make of All This?

You are probably thinking by now; this has been an interesting discussion (or so I hope), but so what? Why should I care whether God has a council of heavenly beings or not? Does this have any relevance to me? And is there any practical worth to such a discussion? These are all fair questions. So why did God choose to give us these fleeting glimpses into heaven? After reviewing the previous mentioned passages, I believe the evidence strongly suggests that God utilizes a council of divine beings to aid Him in the administration of His justice. Because He is omniscient and omnipresent, I do not believe He needs it, but it teaches some fundamental truths about our God. His judgments are not arbitrary or tyrannical. He desires to hear the input of others. His first inclination is not wrath but the search for truth. The reporting of His vigilant angels conveys that nothing escapes God's notice.[76] His rulings are made only after thoughtful deliberation. Through patience and hopeful warnings, God's mercy seeks repentance rather than the execution of His judgments. Collectively, these observations draw a picture of a God who is fair and upright in His judgments. Trusting that God will be fair to us is a serious matter of faith. To strengthen our faith in Him, perhaps God chose to give us a glimpse into His council to show His honorable approach to justice. Like the psalmist of old, He wants us to hold dear that "He will judge the world in righteousness" and "execute judgment for the peoples with equity" (Psalm 9:8). Take it to heart, we have a righteous Judge.

Because God's character is deeply rooted in justice, He expects His people to develop this trait as well. Micah bluntly told the people of Judah what God expected of them; "He has told you, O man, what is good; And what does the LORD require of you But to do justice, to love kindness, And to walk humbly with your God?" (Micah 6:8). Sometimes we need a wake-up call from a Micah. Could you handle the frankness? Following the letter of the Law without incorporating its essence into one's character had created a morally complacent people which appalled God. Similarly, Jesus accused the Pharisees of nitpicking the lesser important aspects of the Law while neglecting "the weightier provisions of the law; justice and mercy and faithfulness" (Matthew 23:23). Like the "swoosh" symbol universally identifies the Nike brand, just deeds should distinguish the Christian. Christianity and unfairness together is like a zebra with polka-dots – it just isn't right.

Opportunities to treat others fairly pervade all areas of life, especially in business. After reminding Judah to walk in the ways of justice, Micah shared an admonition from God concerning unfair business practices; "Is there yet a man in the wicked house, Along with the treasures of wickedness And a short measure that is cursed? Can I justify wicked scales And a bag of deceptive weights?" (Micah 6:10-11). God considers the exploitation of others through misleading business practices as wicked. Can you recall any deceptive marketing practices that lured you into considering a particular product? It was not too long ago that a proliferation of deceptive nutritional claims about food items, like being "low fat," caused the FDA to sponsor legislation to curb such practices. What a sad state of affairs when marketing norms of some companies become so corrupt that the government needs to step in and regulate an industry.

It works both ways though. How do you conduct business? Are your measures fair? Do you accomplish your work assignments in a productive fashion? Do you accurately depict the time you work on your time sheet? What other ways might you exploit your employer? Someone shared with me a story of an individual who bought a car through the money gained from falsifying their time sheet. God considers such "measures" cursed and wicked.

Have you ever overreacted to an incident which resulted in unfair consequences? I think we all have experienced this failing at some point in our lives. When my son was very young, I remember really letting him have it for some form of mischievous behavior. "I'll teach him," I thought, as I immediately levied a harsh punishment on him. Later, my wife made me aware of the broader circumstances that precipitated his misdeeds. He had still done wrong, but my ranting and raving and inappropriate punishment did not fit the crime. Apologizing to my son for my hasty reaction was a very awkward parental moment. As difficult as it was, I let him know that I had misjudged the situation and needed to lessen his punishment because I had treated him unfairly. Consulting my wife before jumping to a specific conclusion would have been the wiser course of action. Remember, justice seeks truth which may require patience, but haughty presumption promotes wrath and injustice.

God's practice of using the divine council to help Him rule and bring about justice should cause us to mull over some questions. Do any practical applications exist that would be advantageous for the church today? Can groups somehow serve church leadership by providing counsel or advice in order to help them be successful? Peter tells elders not to lord "over those allotted to your charge" (1 Peter 5:3). Unilateral changes and decisions by church leadership will often cause feelings of imposition to arise among members. To justify conducting business in such a fashion, many leaders would claim that "they have a finger on the pulse of the congregation." Experience has taught me otherwise. Church folk tend to find change difficult, so what people hold dear to their hearts should be thoroughly understood. Leaders who act presumptuously risk diminishing their ability to lead effectively.

For a number of years, I was privileged to serve on the Florida A&M/Florida State University's College of Engineering Advisory Board. This group was chartered to review the current activities and new undertakings of the College and provide helpful advice and observations to the dean. One important attribute in forming this board was its diversity. Group membership included an array of expertise from across industry, politics, government, and academia. This diverse group brought to the dean a rich array of perspectives which helped to remove the biases of any particular faction. But better yet, it often coalesced in a synergistic fashion and provided guidance to the dean that would not have been derived by any of the particular parties alone. Leadership in our churches would serve their congregations well if they occasionally brought together a diverse mix of members from across the congregation to gather their impressions on current activities and potential future changes. Remember, it is only information and advice. I have learned the hard way over the years; you cannot manage what you don't know. Solomon believed ample advice correlates to the success of our undertakings; "Without consultation, plans are frustrated, But with many counselors they succeed" (Proverbs 15:22).

When leadership believes a new initiative or a particular change is in order, a committee may be a useful tool when chartered properly. A larger span of the church's membership can be directly touched by their investigations. Leadership, in most cases, should maintain the responsibility for final decisions, but a good committee can bring to the leadership team a variety of options with pros and cons and a final recommendation. For example, I have seen preacher search committees ease the burden of the monumental charge of selecting a new preacher. Such a committee could solicit multiple sources for candidates, review the applicants' qualifications per guidelines from the leadership team, and recommend a short list of individuals for a tryout.

Good guidance, leadership, and communication are a must for the success of a committee. A committee that reflects a good cross-section of the congregation and is diligent in their efforts to do the right thing will help bring buy-in to the final decision. Delegating will also promote growth in the individual committee members, thus allowing the experience to serve as a training ground for future leaders. Committees are obviously not always necessary or warranted, but they can aid in producing willing followers. As Peter wisely teaches, even elders should not serve begrudgingly (1 Peter 5:2); so we should avoid, where practical, the need to have our brothers and sisters follow begrudgingly. God seeks fairness and justice in His decisions and so should church leadership. Whatever scheme appears appropriate for arriving at a decision, God's will must ultimately be sought.

One of the saddest things I've heard during my many years of association with churches came from two elders. They told me that the members of their congregation rarely gave them input on anything. What an alarming situation. Rather than exploring potential reasons for this or resultant concerns, I would like to take us in a different direction. We, as members of local congregations, need to communicate with leadership. Whatever you do, please do not just complain about what you do not like. Be gracious and respectful to your leaders and let them know what you believe is going well. Like all of us, leaders need positive reinforcement for their hard work and successes. Our concerns should be conveyed with grace and have the church's best interest in mind. Personal preferences should be made known, while always keeping in mind that Christ's goal for His church is not about pleasing us. However, if enough members voice a personal preference about something, the leadership team may want to reconsider the current approach. Most of all, provide constructive inputs on how ministry can be more effective, and like the spirit in Micaiah's vision who stepped forward, be ready to serve. Such communication will facilitate fairness and equity in your leaders' decisions.

More significantly, God desires our input. He wants to hear from us. God's purposes will not be thwarted, but our prayers become effective when they align with His will (1 John 5:14). Typically in life, many pathways can lead us to the same destination. In Micaiah's vision, God decided Ahab was to fall at Ramoth-gilead, but the angels debated over the "pathway" to reach this objective. The spirit's suggestion provided just one of many options to accomplish God's will. Be specific with your prayers. Let God know your feelings and preferences about the life situations that you, others, and your church may be facing. God knows the end game. If our prayers align with His will, He may honor our requests. Unfortunately, not all pathways lead to the same place, so sometimes our limited view, or the personal nature of the circumstances, may cause us to lose objectivity with where God may be going with things. Nevertheless, God at times relents and changes His plans. Hezekiah became mortally ill, and Isaiah prophesied to him that the illness would take his life. Hezekiah fell on the mercy of the Lord and wept bitterly before Him in prayer (2 Kings 20:1-6). Before Isaiah could leave the premises, God relented and told Isaiah to report to Hezekiah that fifteen years would be added to his life. God obviously cares deeply about our requests, because He placed His Spirit in us to give depth of meaning to our prayers (Romans 8:26). I only can sum it up one way; pray, pray, pray; God loves us and wants us to lay our desires at His feet.

Questions

1. Can you recall any situations in life where you believe you were treated unfairly? What do you think was the cause of the unfair treatment? How did this make you feel?

2. Why is it important that we believe God is just? What if God was not fair? How might that affect you?

3. What does Nebuchadnezzar's judgment teach us? How does revering God and praising Him produce humility?

4. What do you think were the most important points in determining whether the divine council is real? What concerns might oppose such a conclusion?

5. Why does God give us a glimpse of the divine council? How is it relevant to us today?

6. Consider all the passages related to the divine council. What do they teach us about God?

7. Do you believe any practical applications for use in the church today can be derived from God's use of a divine council? Explain.

8. As a Christian, have you given much thought to being fair to others? What areas of your life present the most opportunities for exhibiting just behavior? Are you ever tempted to go against this virtue? What prompts this behavior? How should these actions be addressed?

9. How does receiving counsel help us be fairer to others? What concerns might exist when receiving counsel? How might we counteract such concerns?

Chapter 9

Angels and God's Judgment

And I heard the angel of the waters saying,
"Righteous are You, who are and who were, O Holy One,
because You judged these things (Revelation 16:5).

In 2004, Lion's Gate Entertainment released the film *The Punisher*. Based on a Marvel Comic book series, the main character adopted the title "The Punisher" because of the form of vigilante justice he administered. Typical of many Hollywood productions, the movie sought to bring us alongside the afflicted and join them in a deep-seated animosity against the heartless oppressors. At the beginning of the film, a crime lord's son was killed in an illegal weapons deal that was foiled by the FBI. Of course the crime lord wanted revenge. After uncovering the identity of the responsible FBI agent, Frank Castle; the crime lord sent a goon squad to execute Castle's entire family while they were at a reunion in a remote area of Puerto Rico. All of Castle's family was murdered, but he miraculously escaped death. A local recluse found Castle barely clinging to life and nursed him back to health. When the recluse returned him to the location of the reunion, he told Castle to "Go with God." Castle vengefully responded, "God's gonna sit this one out." He then headed off to wreak mayhem and destruction on the crime lord's empire and family. To justify his actions, Castle offered the following explanation:

In certain extreme situations, the law is inadequate. In order to shame its inadequacy, it is necessary to act outside the law to pursue natural justice. This is not vengeance. Revenge is not a valid motive, it's an emotional response. No, not vengeance – Punishment!

Obviously, the filmmakers made a feeble attempt at rationalizing away the biblical principle of never taking "your own revenge" (Romans 12:19). Typical of the entertainment industry, this movie left out the greater principles God wants us to adhere to. Evil can easily overcome us when we take on the task of doling out justice to those who mistreat us; that is why God desires us to "overcome evil with good" (v. 21).

Our culture's short-term view of life can pervert the way we look at things. God takes an eternal perspective. Our knowledge of events and other's motives is incomplete and viewed through our own biases. God is all-knowing and has a non-biased view of life's circumstances. God also knows our propensity to become consumed with vengeful scheming that can produce all sorts of evil desires within us. So when assaulted in life, God wants the vengeance left to Him: " 'Vengeance is mine, I will repay,' says the Lord" (Romans 12:19). Along with overcoming evil with good, God's desire for us is to learn self-discipline, forgiveness, and peaceful approaches to dealing with oppressors (v. 18).

God's approach to justice may not always sit well with us. We want immediate action, but our longsuffering God may have other goals in mind. Where others spend eternity may depend on His patience. Nevertheless, most of us would have a hard time relating to the feelings of those who have gravely suffered at the hands of others. I could not imagine my own reaction to someone taking the life of my wife or one of my children. While at NASA, my ill feelings toward a couple of problematic employees created within me the desire to assign them to flame trench monitor duties. Sorry for the space lingo, but the flame trench monitor (fictitious of course) observes main engine ignition from inside the trench that safely directs the rocket exhaust away from the vehicle. Not a very good place to be during launch. Seriously though, Scripture is clear about the administration of justice for wrongs done against us; leave it up to God. Civil authorities serve Him as a ministry to achieve justice whether they realize it or not (Romans 13:3-4). And if justice is not served in this lifetime, God will see to it when Christ returns. Eternity is a long time.

Scripture provides a unique picture of God judicially at work in several temporal events where His angels were miraculously and providentially used to carry out His judgments. A quick survey of the stories of Sodom and Gomorrah, Sennacherib's assault on Jerusalem, and the death of Herod Agrippa I will aid our understanding of God's just nature. The angels will also be very busy at the Second Coming of Christ. We will turn to their activity in this glorious, yet dire, time to further appreciate our Lord's righteous approach to judgment.

Undercover Angels

Looking for an angel story to develop a new action movie? I vote for the story of Sodom and Gomorrah. This one fits Hollywood to a tee: drama, action, mystery, destruction, and moral corruption. What an intriguing story, as well as a great place for us to investigate God's attribute of justice. In Genesis 18, God and two men (identified as angels in Genesis 19:1) visit Abraham by the oaks of Mamre. During their conversation, God revealed to Abraham that "[t]he outcry of Sodom and Go-

> The Hebrew term translated as "outcry" has legal overtones, indicating a plea for help from those who are enduring a horrible injustice. [77]

morrah is indeed great, and their sin is exceedingly grave" (18:20). Because of the gravity of the situation, the Lord determined a divine investigation was necessary to validate the severity of the outcry, so the two angels headed for Sodom to perform some detective work.

Abraham was probably well aware of Sodom and Gomorrah's evil reputation. Lot, Abraham's nephew, had previously sojourned with him from Ur to Canaan. After settling in that region, both their herds flourished, so Lot decided to relocate to the lush Jordan valley adjacent to Sodom. At this juncture of the Genesis story, the author raised a red warning flag; "Now the men of Sodom were wicked exceedingly and sinners against the LORD" (Genesis 13:13). So Abraham understood the destiny of Sodom and Gomorrah could not be good, and his beloved nephew's fate may have been at stake. Knowing the angels would encounter wanton unrighteousness at Sodom, Abraham believed that he must act quickly on Lot's behalf. Like a countdown for the righteous; fifty, forty-five, forty, thirty, twenty, or ten, Abraham appealed to God's just nature to save the righteous within these wicked cities (18:24-32).

> Far be it from You to do such a thing, to slay the righteous with the wicked, so that the righteous and the wicked are treated alike. Far be it from You! Shall not the Judge of all the earth deal justly? (v. 25).

God assured Abraham that even for the sake of ten righteous He would not destroy the cities.

Arriving at Sodom in the evening, undercover operations for the angels commenced (Genesis 19). None the wiser to the angels' identity, Lot graciously greeted them at the city gate and invited them to stay at his home. Prior to turning in for the night, men of all ages from every part of the city surrounded Lot's home demanding he turn over his guests, so they could have sexual relations with them. Have you ever seen a situation where the unbridled practice of sin became the norm for a large group of

Based on usage outside the Bible, the word translated as "blindness" in Genesis 19:11 appears to indicate that the angels struck the men with a sudden flash of light that caused temporary blindness.[78]

people? Gross sexual depravity had overtaken virtually the entire city of Sodom. As Lot pleaded with the Sodomites on behalf of his guests, the scene erupted into imminent violence. God's holy angels witnessed enough. They revealed their heavenly identity by striking "the men who were at the doorway of the house with blindness" and pulled Lot into the safety of the house (vv.10-11). Groping around in the dark, some of the Sodomites now experience total blindness – both physical and spiritual.

Confirming the outcry's accuracy, and no longer burdened by their secret identities, the angels began to speak with the authority of God. They directed Lot to gather his family and escape from the city. The angels made sure Lot understood the urgency of the situation; "For we are about to destroy this place, because their outcry has become so great before the LORD that the LORD has sent us to destroy it" (Genesis 19:13). When morning dawned, Lot apparently either struggled with the incredible doomsday prediction or patiently hoped other relatives would join him (note vv. 12, 14), because he hesitated to leave Sodom. The angels could not allow him to dillydally any longer; "So the men [angels] seized his hand and the hand of his wife and the hands of his two daughters, for the compassion of the LORD was upon him; and they brought him out, and put him outside the city" (v. 16). Promising not to destroy the city of Zoar, one of the angels granted Lot's request to take refuge in this fortunate town. Once Lot and his family were outside ground zero, God rained fire and brimstone on Sodom and Gomorrah, utterly reducing them to ashes (2 Peter 2:6).

Jude and Peter both comment on the immoral nature of the sin that led to Sodom and Gomorrah's destruction (Jude 1:7; 2 Peter 2:6-8), yet God, through the prophet Ezekiel, made this comment about the corrupt character of these cities:

> ... Sodom: she and her daughters had arrogance, abundant food and careless ease, but she did not help the poor and needy. Thus they were haughty and committed

abominations before Me. Therefore I removed them when
I saw it (Ezekiel 16:49-50).

Obviously, Sodom and Gomorrah's sin was multi-faceted which
should not be unexpected. Once a particular area of our character collapses, the next will tend to fall much easier. It is worth making two brief observations concerning our involvement in these
types of sins. First, I believe sexual sins are a huge problem in the
church today. I have worked with several individuals in this regard
and am aware of numerous other situations that have taken down
many happy marriages and destroyed the good virtue of others.
Many sexual sins today are precipitated by pornography. This
problem is exacerbated by the many venues that facilitate viewing
it in secrecy and anonymity. Not only are many sexual sins shame-
lessly promoted, but pornography insidiously perverts God's design for the sexual relationship between married couples. What
was meant for intimacy and romance is replaced with raw sex. Individuals hooked on porn tend to progress into worse sins affect-
ing the innocent along the way. Given the chance, the flames of
lust that arise from porn can easily overwhelm even the most devout Christian. Sodom and Gomorrah started somewhere; if you
have a problem with this sin – run for help. Fast!

Second, God's disdain for Sodom and Gomorrah's ill-treatment
of the poor stands just as relevant today as it did in Abraham's
time. Many refer to this as God's concern about social injustice.
Right along with idolatry, the prophets trumpeted numerous warnings about treating the poor unfairly. God has so richly blessed
many of us. To then blindly, even arrogantly, ignore the plight of
the poor is unjust in God's eyes. He desires us to bless others in
need from the abundance He has graciously blessed us with
(2 Corinthians 8:14). Our just God wants us to treat others fairly,
and this includes taking care of the poor. Several years ago, I remember helping my wife with a hungry man who stopped by the
church in search of food. We offered him a number of things from
the pantry, but he humbly declined taking too much. He wanted

to make sure ample food was available for the next hungry visitor. What a great heart! He could have taken the food and sold it, but he empathized with others in dire need. Time for a heart check – the Christian's heart should be compassionately moved to action by the difficulties of the poor. Otherwise, at best, such a heart should be considered immature or perhaps even corrupted by the world's vision of accumulating wealth. Sodom and Gomorrah's culture had some similarities to our own. What areas of your life would you consider aligned with American culture? From a Christian perspective, is that good or bad?

At first glance, we may view the story of Sodom and Gomorrah as evidence that the Lord is a God of uncontrolled wrath. Most certainly, His judgment against these cities was executed in a cataclysmic fashion. However, Sodom and Gomorrah's evil did not spring up overnight (Genesis 13:13). God had probably been patient with these cities for some time, but when the outcry of the innocent goes up, He acts. It is reminiscent of God responding to Israel's cry for help when their bondage under the Egyptians turned exceedingly cruel (Exodus 2:23-25). Illustrating God's concern for how evil maligns His truth and seeks to exploit the righteous, Peter described the overwhelming burden faced by Lot while living among the unbridled evil of the Sodomites;

> and if He rescued righteous Lot, oppressed by the sensual conduct of unprincipled men (for by what he saw and heard that righteous man, while living among them, felt his righteous soul tormented day after day by their lawless deeds), then the Lord knows how to rescue the godly from temptation, and to keep the unrighteous under punishment for the day of judgment (2 Peter 2:7-9).

God hears the prayers of the oppressed. When you feel pressured by others to participate in sinful activities, pray to be rescued. God's will is for you to be delivered from such unrighteousness.

The Sodom and Gomorrah narrative also demonstrates how God's judgments are not arbitrary. He sent angels covertly into Sodom to validate the severity of the outcry. Not until His divine agents witnessed the sexual corruption was the judgment declared. Remembering Abraham's plea (Genesis 19:29), God removed righteous Lot and members of his family from the city. In fact, the angels' abrupt response to Lot's hesitation to leave the city was because "the compassion of the LORD was upon him" (v. 16). This is not a picture of a God who sought wrath, but a God who fairly dealt with a deplorable situation. Sin's injustice produced the great human outcry. God's intention for humanity had been corrupted by unrestrained unrighteousness. A judgment of death was justified to stop any further spread of such depravity, providing a lesson for the ages as to God's intention for humanity.

Sennacherib Versus the Angel of the Lord

Sennacherib's invasion of Judah serves as additional interesting subject matter that we can use to evaluate God's justice (2 Kings 18:13-19:37). During Hezekiah's reign in Judah, Sennacherib, king of Assyria, captured all of Judah's fortified cities and demanded the surrender of Jerusalem. Sennacherib's rationale for their submission included bold mocking accusations against the God of Judah: the Lord could not be trusted to deliver them (18:30), the king of Assyria was mightier than Judah's God (vv. 33-35), and God would deceive them (19:10). In almost any story or movie today, such blatant disregard to someone signals what's coming next – vindication. Hebrew storytelling appears to be no different as this narrative approached its climax. Hezekiah not only prayed to God for deliverance but requested that their rescue occur in such a fashion "that all the kingdoms of the earth may know that You alone, O LORD, are God" (v. 19). Ramifications to our prayers can often be far reaching; Hezekiah probably had no idea what awaited the Assyrian army.

God wasted no time in sending a response to Hezekiah's prayer through the prophet Isaiah. God first acknowledged the importance of Hezekiah's request; "Because you have prayed to Me ... I have heard you" (2 Kings 19:20). We should never underestimate the power of sincere prayer. God highlighted two major offenses by Sennacherib prior to declaring His judgment. Concerning Sennacherib's arrogant speech, God contemptuously stated, "Whom have you reproached and blasphemed? And against whom have you raised your voice, And haughtily lifted your eyes? Against the Holy One of Israel!" (v. 22). Next, Sennacherib's self-promoting words from the past came back to haunt him. Through directly quoting the Assyrian king, God illustrated how Sennacherib's heart could only produce self-glorifying speech for his past accomplishments. It was all about his greatness; there was no room to glorify God in Sennacherib's heart. Rebuking the king's high and mighty claims, God emphatically pointed out that He was responsible for the outcomes of these achievements, not Sennacherib: "Have you not heard? Long ago I did it; from ancient times I planned it Now I have brought it to pass" (v. 25). Sennacherib was but a pawn in the panoply of God's providential workings.

Perhaps the easiest vice for leaders to fall prey to is arrogance. Many facets of leadership can feed a vulnerable ego in an unhealthy way. Newfound power, ingratiating employees (or followers), recognition, and various types of perks and other accolades make the best of us susceptible to developing an arrogant disposition. Nebuchadnezzar, Sennacherib, and Herod Agrippa I all succumbed to this moral fault. Rather than becoming humble servant-leaders that facilitate the success of others, leaders often want to be placed on a pedestal for all to honor and obey. Abusing their authority, one-upping those standing in their way and taking undue credit for the work of others are just a few of the tactics used to feed their self-aggrandizing agendas.

A number of years ago, a situation arose between my office and an "opposing" office that had competing solutions. Pros and cons of the potential resolutions were being bantered back and forth but no agreement was forthcoming. To try to resolve the matter, we had an internal meeting to get our ducks in a row because those in my own office had differing opinions on what the appropriate course of action should be. I remember that a co-worker explained his point of view to the group, after which he stated that his proposed solution "was the right thing to do." What transpired next left a lasting impression on me. Our most senior manager in the room retorted, "I do not care about what is right anymore, I just want to win!" His decision-making faculties had become so twisted by arrogance that right and wrong took second fiddle to how he would be viewed by others. Selecting a wrong solution was OK to him, as long as the outcome portrayed him as the victor. What a sad approach to viewing things! This potential role model fell several notches in my eyes that day. I found his egotistical attitude so repugnant that I internally swore to always resist such a horrendous character flaw. With God's contempt for arrogant behavior, I suppose, in a strange way, that I am indebted to this manager's bad example.

Sennacherib's offenses had serious theological overtones. Was God truly mightier than the great king of Assyria, and the pagan gods that stood behind him? Could God defend His people or should they be allied with the Assyrian gods? As God pronounced judgment against Sennacherib, these questions must be satisfactorily addressed.

> Because of your raging against Me, and because your arrogance has come up to My ears, Therefore I will put My hook in your nose, And My bridle in your lips, And I will turn you back by the way which you came. ... Therefore thus says the LORD concerning the king of Assyria, "He shall not come to this city or shoot an arrow there; and he will not come before it with a shield or throw up a siege ramp against it. By the way that he came, by the same he shall return, and he shall not come to this city," declares the LORD (2 Kings 19:28, 32-33).

To the Assyrians, such words would probably have sounded like an inflated and unsubstantiated wartime rant. How could the lowly Judeans turn back the ominous army of the Assyrians? To answer Hezekiah's prayer that the Lord alone should be recognized as God, an extraordinary event would be required.[79] Sennacherib entered Judah as a destroyer, but God sent a destroying angel to crush the Assyrian army.

> Then it happened that night that the angel of the LORD went out and struck 185,000 in the camp of the Assyrians; and when men rose early in the morning, behold, all of them were dead. So Sennacherib king of Assyria departed and returned home, and lived at Nineveh (vv. 35-36).

Reminiscent of the devastating death of the firstborn of Egypt, God left no doubt as to who was the one and true God.

God's judgment was swift and harsh; but in defending His sovereignty, integrity, as well as His innocent people, God proved to be just for His actions in this story. The evil empire of Assyria would no longer be a threat to Judah. The mighty heavenly being that inflicted such a devastating blow on the Assyrian army appeared only briefly in the story. He was but a creation and servant of the Almighty. In no uncertain terms, the Lord answered Hezekiah's prayer so that all may know that God, and only God, was the One to be united with.

Herod, an Angel, and Worms

In Chapter 7 we noted that King Herod Agrippa I had executed James the apostle and intended the same fate for Peter (Acts 12:1-4). Because of the fervent prayer of the church, God sent an angel to miraculously rescue Peter from prison. After executing the guards for their supposed incompetence for allowing Peter's escape, Herod traveled to Caesarea, the capital city of the province. A scheduled public address by Herod will serve as the final setting for our evaluation of God's justice (vv. 21-23).

To look the part of a king, Herod wore his "royal apparel" for his speech (Acts 12:21). Have you ever been fooled about a person's abilities because of his or her appearance? I have learned my lesson a couple times. Some sure look the part, but once you start to query them you quickly ask, "Where's the beef?" A puppet king of the Roman government, Herod needed all the help he could get. Josephus provided additional detail to Herod's luxurious attire, and its impression upon the crowd:

> He put on a garment made wholly of silver, and of a contexture truly wonderful, and came into the theater early in the morning; at which time the silver of his garment being illuminated by the fresh reflection of the sun's rays upon it, shone out after a surprising manner, and was so resplendent as to spread horror over those that looked intently upon him; and presently his flatterers cried out ... that he was a god.[80]

Luke recorded that the people cried out, "The voice of a god and not of a man!" (v. 22). To accept accolades of this nature was inexcusable for a Jew.[81] God condemned to death the ruler of Tyre for elevating himself to such a lofty status.

> ... Because your heart is lifted up And you have said, "I am a god, I sit in the seat of gods, In the heart of the seas'; Yet you are a man and not God, Although you make your heart like the heart of God" (Ezekiel 28:2).

> "You will die the death of the uncircumcised By the hand of strangers, For I have spoken!" declares the Lord GOD! (v. 10).

With offenses already accumulating against His people, God wasted no time in casting a judgment against Herod; "And immediately an angel of the Lord struck him because he did not give

God the glory, and he was eaten by worms and died" (Acts 12:23). According to Josephus, Herod felt a violent pain arise in his belly and stated, "I, whom you call a god, am commanded presently to depart this life; while Providence thus reproves the lying words you just now said to me; and I, who was by you called an immortal, am immediately to be hurried away by death."[82] Even while facing death, Herod's proud demeanor would curtail him from showing humility and accepting blame for receiving the glory that was only due God. Instead, he pointed to the crowd's words, not his own heart.

Not seen by anyone, the angel executed God's providential judgment. There was no grand display or immediacy to the outcome, as was the case with Sodom and Gomorrah and Sennacherib's army, for Herod's ailment took five days to accomplish its goal.[83] Our just God freed the early church from a violent oppressor. Herod's arrogance would have continued to feed on the pleasing responses of the Jews as he persecuted Christ's fledgling church (Acts 12:3). Herod's deity-accepting nature signed his death warrant. The Almighty Judge had seen enough.

> The text does not specifically state that God pronounced the judgment. However, nowhere in Scripture do we see angels independently casting judgments with such severe consequences. Even the archangel Michael knew it was not his place to pronounce a judgment against Satan over Moses' body (Jude 1:9). Thus, I feel it safe to say that Herod's judgment was from God.

Rescuers

A similar pattern existed between the judgments against Sodom and Gomorrah, Sennacherib, and Herod. God heard the outcry of the oppressed, arrogance was exhibited, angel(s) delivered the righteous, and a horrifying judgment was executed. What I would like to draw our attention to is God's rescue of the oppressed. In these events, God sent angels to deliver His people, but we are not to sit and wait for God to send angels to those in need. God has given us the ability today to be rescuers. Oppressed by a sinful world, many desperately need a deliverer.

About ten years ago, my wife and I encountered an unusual situation in the Blue Ridge Mountains. We had just finished a hike to Crabtree Falls and were walking back to our car. We had to park quite a distance from the trailhead because the access road was closed. As we started to go downhill, our pace began to quicken, when all of a sudden we heard the anxious sounds of birds chirping and the fluttering of wings. The commotion appeared to be coming from a storm drain off to our left. As we peered down through the heavy iron grating, we saw two little birds that had become trapped and were frantically trying to escape their new found prison.

The birds must have noticed some good tasting bugs in the storm drain. Not knowing any better, they made themselves sleek by holding their wings close to their bodies and hopped through the slots in the grating. I am sure they enjoyed their meal, but when it was time to leave their dining room, they could not hop high enough to get through the grate. They needed to use their wings, but with their wings unfurled they could not make it through the slots in the grating. Their once scrumptious dining room had become their prison. To free the birds, we cleared away the overgrowth of grass from around the edges of the grate and dug out years of encrusted gunk that held the heavy prison bars in place. With both of us tugging at it for quite some time, the grate finally broke loose, and we were able to remove the grating. Apprehensively watching us through the whole ordeal, the birds quickly escaped to live another day. We were exhausted from the day's activities, but the excitement of the rescue revitalized us. Incredible warmth now engulfed us as we continued our trek to the car. What a wonderful feeling!

Just like our chirping friends, sometimes we humans jump into the storm drains of life only to realize that we cannot get out. Addictions, deep-seated lust, greed, envy, etc., hold us captive. We may actually try to escape but weaknesses overwhelm our good intentions only to fall again. Imprisoned in a world of sin, some urgently await gracious rescuers to offer them a helping hand. Jude directly appeals to our compassionate hearts to help liberate them; "And have mercy on some, who are doubting; save others, snatching them out of the fire; and on some have mercy with fear, hating even the garment polluted by the flesh" (Jude 1:22-23). They need to be befriended, temptations removed, placed in a safe place, and held accountable. Some may need special assistance; we need to help them find it. Most of all, Christ needs to be introduced (or reintroduced) into their lives. Jesus not only provides healing, He offers a hope that they can change, and a hope they will spend eternity with Him in heaven. Too many churches today are inept at developing rescuers. We become focused on the periphery areas of Christianity and neglect the spiritually productive ones. So much is at stake. Outside Christ, all fall short (Romans 3:23). Were you not offered a helping hand at some point in life? Is it not time you reached out to help someone else?

Final Judgment

Would it not be interesting to understand the daily routine of a typical angel? Scripture only provides an occasional glimpse into their activities, usually at major events. Perhaps some day we will work side-by-side with angels on some heavenly task. But to experience such a prospect, we will need to make it through the Final Judgment. According to God's Word, this will be an exceptionally busy period for the angels. Because the Final Judgment is an extensive topic, I will integrate Matthew's portrayal of it, which will suffice to draw some reasonable conclusions as to God's just nature.

Shortly before the crucifixion, Jesus shared with His disciples a parable concerning the judgment (Matthew 25:31-46). Upon His glorious return, Jesus will bring with Him "all the angels" (v. 31). Once Jesus sits on His throne, the Judgment will commence. All nations will be brought before Him, and Jesus will separate the sheep (the righteous) from the goats (the unrighteous). We would assume the angels actually perform the gathering and the physical (or perhaps spiritual) separation; but to explicitly determine this, we must refer to some of Jesus' earlier teachings.

After telling the parable of the tares among wheat with its cryptic imagery of some of the events at the Final Judgment (Matthew 13:24-30), Jesus clarified its symbolism to His disciples (vv. 36-43). Jesus explained that He sows the wheat (sons of the kingdom), while the devil sows the tares (sons of the evil one). Jesus noted that the angels are the reapers, but they will not fulfill their role of removing the tares until the Judgment. Concerning this activity, Jesus more explicitly stated

> The Son of Man will send forth His angels, and they will gather out of His kingdom all stumbling blocks, and those who commit lawlessness, and will throw them into the furnace of fire; in that place there will be weeping and gnashing of teeth (vv. 41-42).

This parable teaches that during the Final Judgment, the angels will gather the unrighteous and execute the judgment declared by Jesus upon these lawless offenders. In the language of the two parables – the tares are burned; the goats receive eternal punishment. But what of the righteous? Do the angels have a role concerning them? During a separate discussion, Jesus fills the void left by the parable of tares among wheat by providing a complementary statement for gathering the righteous; "And He will send forth His angels with a great trumpet and they will gather together His elect from the four winds, from one end of the sky to the other" (Matthew 24:31).

With the tares removed and the righteous assembled together, Jesus will bestow the reward that awaits His godly ones; "Then the righteous will shine forth as the sun in the kingdom of their Father" (Matthew 13:43). So in the case of the righteous, the angels will gather and assemble them before Jesus, and He will declare that they are to permanently inherit the kingdom. Again, per the language of the two parables – the wheat will be gathered into Christ's barn; the sheep will receive eternal life.

In the case of the Final Judgment, I hope you noted that God the Son (Jesus) represents the Godhead as Judge. Jesus will send the angels out to gather all the people, and the separation will take place by His judgment. The angels will only execute the orders of the righteous Judge. In the Gospel of John, Jesus attested to the fact that the Father "gave Him authority to execute judgment" (John 5:27). However, Jesus further explained that His judgments will not be of His own doing but will be based on the will of His Father; "My judgment is just, because I do not seek My own will, but the will of Him who sent Me" (v. 30). God the Father and God the Son will be perfectly aligned when it comes to judging humanity for their deeds.

In his second letter to the Thessalonians, Paul utilized the reality of the Final Judgment to instill hope into this persecuted church (2 Thessalonians 1:3-10). Steadfast faith in Christ in the face of sufferings would allow them to be "considered worthy of the kingdom of God" (v. 5). But knowing more ill-treatment was on the horizon, you can imagine the questions and concerns these beleaguered Christians had. What was the basis for such hope? What assurance do we have of such a promise? If the righteous are unjustly treated by their persecutors in this life, what will be different about the Judgment? Should we continue on this dreadful path? To ground their hope in the Final Judgment, Paul stated it would be a "righteous judgment" (v. 5). Driving this concept home, he explained

For after all it is only just for God to repay with affliction those who afflict you, and to give relief to you who are afflicted and to us as well when the Lord Jesus will be revealed from heaven with His mighty angels in flaming fire, dealing out retribution to those who do not know God and to those who do not obey the gospel of our Lord Jesus. These will pay the penalty of eternal destruction, away from the presence of the Lord and from the glory of His

power, when He comes to be glorified in His saints on that
day, and to be marveled at among all who have believed –
for our testimony to you was believed (vv. 6-10).

For the Thessalonians and us today, we can muster great hope in
the fact that God and Jesus will act justly in accordance with their
promises at the Final Judgment. We may not be able to predict how
things will work out in the short term, but when the Judgment is
upon us, God's prophetic words will come to pass as promised.

The separation caused by sin has left the angels with the harsh
task of executing the future judgment on the unrighteous. Unlike
the angels of contemporary thought, they will not be revealed at
the Judgment as soft, unassuming creatures. Amid the holy fire of
heaven, these mighty beings will be an unwelcome and terrifying
sight to the unrighteous as they deal out retribution. Yet even while
imagining such a melancholy scene, one is drawn to God's righteousness through His fateful warnings. We are plainly told that the
punished will be the unrighteous (goats), sons of the evil one
(tares), lawless, stumbling blocks, afflicters, and disobedient, as
well as those portrayed as not knowing God and rejecting Jesus.
The rewarded shall be the righteous (sheep), sons of the kingdom
(wheat), elect, afflicted, and obedient, whose faith in Christ makes
them worthy. In the parable of the sheep and goats (Matthew
25:31-46), salvation comes to those who perform righteous acts of
compassion, while those who lack compassion and are self-seeking and complacent toward others are destroyed.

By amply distinguishing the two pathways and giving us the
ability to achieve righteousness, God stands fair and just in judging our eventual choices. Nothing exemplifies God's just nature
more than the sacrificial sending of His Son. Because we are helpless to erase the guilt sin imposes upon us, Christ's blood enables
God to declare us innocent. Accepting the cleansing power of
Christ's blood allows us to enter into a relationship with our holy
God. For those who do not choose to be cleansed by the blood
of Christ, their sinful state will keep them from taking part in God's

holy kingdom, and the angels stand ready to separate them from the righteous. God has gone to great extremes. The choice is ours.

Serious stuff! Nevertheless, should we not rejoice and be at peace, knowing God is fair and just? Are we not greatly blessed in God's longsuffering nature as well? Thank goodness He is "patient ... not wishing for any to perish but for all to come to repentance" (2 Peter 3:9). With outstretched arms, our compassionate and just God extends His loving grace to redeem any who are willing, all the way to the end.

Questions

1. Recall a situation in life when you were mistreated by another person. How did you want to respond? How can such situations be spiritually unhealthy for us?

2. Why is God in a better position to administer justice than us? Is it hard to yield this to Him? Why? What Christian principles does God want us to learn/utilize when we are unjustly oppressed?

3. Why did God destroy Sodom and Gomorrah? Why should God be viewed as just for carrying out such a harsh judgment? How does our culture's infatuation with sexuality affect the church today?

4. What was Sennacherib's sin? Why was God just in dealing out such a harsh judgment against the Assyrians?

5. To what vice do you think leaders are most susceptible? What would be the consequences to one's leadership if this vice was routinely exhibited?

6. The angels rescued God's people from some of His temporal judgments. Can we be rescuers today? Who would we rescue? What are we rescuing them from? Do you have someone in mind? How would you go about rescuing them?

7. How will Jesus use the angels during the Final Judgment? What assurance do we have that the Final Judgment will be just?

8. How does the Final Judgment produce hope in the Christian?

9. Integrate the various judgment scenes we have discussed in this chapter. What do they collectively reveal to you about God?

Part 5

Sovereignty of God

Sovereignty Prelude

Living in a society where we can pursue the "American Dream" of prosperity has tremendous advantages. At the same time, I believe an unwanted side effect has taken hold of our culture. With prosperity as our goal in life, the control of others and things that contribute to obtaining our desired destiny becomes paramount. Obviously, many negative consequences could result from such a way of life, such as dehumanizing and manipulating others to achieve our aims. M. Robert Mulholland views our society as "an objectivizing culture ... that views the world primarily as an object 'out there' to be grasped and controlled for our own purposes."[84] Fueled by what our culture views as successful (beauty, money, power, fame, etc.), "Katy bar the door" if we impede another's hard-charging pursuits. Lies, bribes, illicit favors, cheating, and the like have almost become commonplace in an individual's quest to achieve his or her desires. We must ask ourselves, has living in such a culture tainted the Christian's concept of a sovereign God? Have we enthroned "self," giving God the role of facilitator to aid us in attaining our objectives in life? Is it His will or our own that is being sought after? Perhaps Isaiah's warning to Jerusalem cries out to us today:

> You turn things around! Shall the potter be considered as equal with the clay, That what is made should say to its maker, "He did not make me"; Or what is formed say to him who formed it, "He has no understanding?" (Isaiah 29:16).

To untangle our web of cultural influences, it is imperative that we acquaint ourselves with God as ruler.

God's sovereignty refers to His exalted position as absolute and supreme ruler of the universe. Some distinguish His sovereignty as an attribute of His divine nature. However, perhaps it would be

more accurate to differentiate it as a "right that God possesses because of who He is."[85] But why is God granted such a lofty right?
God's perfect attributes undergird His dominion but do they en-
title Him to be declared Sovereign of the universe? Such positional
honor is grounded in one key aspect about God; He is the Creator
of all things. God's powerful word went forth and created our
world and universe out of nothingness (see Genesis 1; Psalms
33:6-9; 148:5; Hebrews 11:3). God's claim to sovereignty over the
entire universe lies in the fact that He is its Creator.

Humankind's relationship to God is as creature to Creator, and
because we were brought into existence by His creative action,
He is our absolute Lord. The psalmist proclaimed that God is also
the rightful owner of His creation;

"The earth is the LORD'S, and all it contains, The world, and
those who dwell in it. For He has founded it upon the seas and established it upon the rivers" (Psalm 24:1-2). Moses also declared,
"Behold, to the LORD your God belong heaven and the highest
heavens, the earth and all that is in it" Deuteronomy 10:14). So as
Creator, God is our Ruler, Lord, and Owner.

Have you ever put together a plastic model and then painted it
to your own satisfaction? Assuming it was your model, you had the
freedom to express your artistic options as you saw fit. If you
wanted to paint your Godzilla model purple, that was your right. It
was your model. As Owner of His creation, God has the freedom
to do with it as He pleases. The psalmist declared, "Whatever the
LORD pleases, He does, In heaven and in earth, in the seas and in
all deeps" (Psalm 135:6). Does that mean that God will act in an arbitrary fashion or with malicious intent toward His creation? You
or I might mischievously paint Godzilla purple, but would God act
in a mischievous manner? Rest assured, God's sovereign actions
come from His holy nature, and He will never do anything contrary to it.[86] Is that not truly freedom, acting consistently with whom
you really are, untainted by external influences?[87] God's steadfast-
ness to His own character assures His creation that its sovereign
King will always rule righteously. What a great blessing to be em-

braced by the Master Potter whose hands unwaveringly are guided by His holy, just, and loving nature. As He spins the potter's wheel, will you take advantage of the goodness He desires to shape for you by becoming pliable clay in His hands? I know that submission is not easy, but understanding God's nature allows me to submit to Him much easier. Let us join Paul in glorifying the loving Ruler of the universe; "He who is the blessed and only Sovereign, the King of kings and Lord of lords ... To Him be honor and eternal dominion! Amen" (1 Timothy 6:15-16).

Chapter 10

Allegiance and Following

The LORD has established His throne in the heavens;
And His sovereignty rules over all (Psalm 103:19).

My thirty-one years with NASA was filled with many blessings. One of the most incredible benefits came from working along-side and observing so many great leaders. Early on, I started to take note of and admire the traits that allowed them to excel in their weighty positions. From my knot-hole, three leadership character-istics separated the superior leaders from the rest of the pack. *Integrity* rose above all the traits in my eyes, because as their superior, your workers need to trust you if you expect them to follow your lead. *Competency* to lead in one's area of responsibility places a close second. Inept lead-ership doesn't command respect and can bring an organization's productivity to a screeching halt. Both of these traits can be de-veloped, but the third has an innate quality. The ability to provide a clear *vision* for the future of an organization is crucial for its sur-vival in our ever-changing world. Lack of vision may result in over-looking the required changes that will keep the organization current and viable. Providing the wrong vision may take a group

> Reflecting on leadership, Astronaut Rick Husband noted the following in his journal, "It's not only about what you do, but what you do next." [88]

down a path that bears no fruit. The skill to be able to envision the appropriate future for an organization is obviously an extremely important gift for a leader to possess.

I remember one leader who was particularly gifted at providing us with a future vision. Unfortunately, his entire management team did not agree with his assessment. Rather than dissenting, a few of them just remained silent. Their subsequent behaviors were not openly subversive, but change was not on their menu. They kept doing the same old things and holding to the same old values. Their lack of commitment to the vision of their leader made the process of change extremely difficult. This demonstrated vividly the importance of allegiance and support to leadership during this time frame. Disloyalty to a leader can create misdirection and chaos among the "troops" and cause the noblest initiatives to fail.

As sovereign Ruler, God deserves our allegiance. He has provided us with a vision for change to become like His Son with the ultimate vision of joining Him for eternity. To accomplish this, He has placed Christ as the leader over the church. We, as members of His church, are to be His followers. Lack of loyalty to God's plans for our future will bring undesirable results to us and possibly others. Observing the allegiance of angels and their relationship to God may help us understand what our roles as followers may entail.

The Position of Angels to God

I would like to briefly revisit three concepts we have already discussed to point out the position of the angels in relationship to God: angels as created beings, angels as servants, and angels in the divine council. We will also evaluate God's title as "Lord of hosts" to determine its implications.

We learned earlier that Psalm 148 identified the angels (v. 2) as created beings. This psalm calls out to all creation to recognize the Lord's sovereign power and authority.[89] All things owe their very existence to the creative force of God's commands (v. 5). Consequently, angels join us as co-creatures of the Creator and in recognizing God as their Ruler, Lord, and Owner. As part of His creation, God uses the angels to achieve His purposes as He pleases. Daniel corroborates this by recording Nebuchadnezzar's recognition of God's sovereignty after the king's experience as a beast of the field; "For His dominion is an everlasting dominion ... He does according to His will in the host of heaven And among the inhabitants of earth" (Daniel 4:34-35). This points out that God's sovereignty is universal.

Angels were also noted as being servants to God in Chapter 2. Psalm 103:19-21 described the angels as servants to the Almighty Lord whose "sovereignty rules over all" (v. 19). Because God is enthroned in the heavens, only praise from the angels befits their mighty Ruler. I have indicated throughout the book how the angels serve God by delivering His messages, executing His judgments, rescuing the righteous, and extending His compassion. Being servants necessitates that angels have a lord. Their lord is God, their sovereign Creator.

In the chapter on the divine council, we again saw the angels in a subservient role to God. In Psalm 89:5-8, the psalmist depicted God as reigning over the divine council. He was revered by the "council of the holy ones" and "above" them all (v. 7). To Israel, the portrayal of God as ruler over the divine council attested to the fact that He reigned over the entire universe.[90] Mighty as the angels were believed to be, God was their unquestioned superior. The throne room scene of Daniel 7:9-10 also succinctly illustrated the relationship of the angels to God. Standing in honor of their sovereign Lord, the heavenly beings who sat upon the lesser thrones waited until God took His seat before they sat down. A theme of angelic service was also portrayed as "[t]housands upon thousands were attending Him, And myriads upon myriads were standing before Him" (v.10). Like courtiers before their King, the angels stood ready to carry out God's will.

A common title for God in the Old Testament was the "Lord of hosts." This title was associated with God's kingship and conveyed His sovereignty over all His hosts. Honoring God in prayer,

Hezekiah lauded Him as the "LORD of hosts, the God of Israel, who is enthroned above the cherubim, You are the God, You alone, of all the kingdoms of the earth. You have made heaven and earth" (Isaiah 37:16). "Hosts" can refer to the angels, but it is also used for a group or army of humans or celestial objects. It appears likely that the title stressed God's unlimited power over both His heavenly and earthly creations.[91] The point is that the angels are hosts, and God is their Lord. When the seraphim declared, "Holy, Holy, Holy, is the LORD of hosts" (6:3), they assuredly included themselves in proclaiming God as their Lord. Most certainly we need to join them in such praise of our God.

The Army of God

The writers of the Old Testament occasionally used language that described God as a powerful warrior. David heartily proclaimed, "Who is the King of Glory? The LORD strong and mighty, the LORD mighty in battle" (Psalm 24:8). Can't you imagine David shouting out this question before his "mighty men," expecting to hear this spirited reply, kind of like a responsive cheer at a pep rally? After the defeat of Pharaoh's army in the Red Sea, Moses' tribute song to God declared that "The LORD is a warrior; The LORD is His name" (Exodus 15:3). Where there is a warrior King, one would expect to find a formidable army, and God's Word often portrays the angels as fulfilling this role.

As Commander-in-Chief, God appointed a commanding officer over His army. Prior to Israel's military campaign against Jericho, Joshua came across a man with his sword drawn at the outskirts of the city (Joshua 5:13-15). Bravely approaching this threatening figure, Joshua asked whether he was friend or foe. In a startling answer, he said, "No; rather I indeed come now as captain of the host of the LORD" (v. 14). Realizing he was in the presence of the commander of God's angelic army, Joshua immediately honored this lauded leader by bowing before him. Joshua then inquisitively asked, "What has my lord to say to his servant?" (v. 14), which creates much anticipation in us twenty-first-century readers, as a forthcoming message from the angelic captain seemed imminent. Regrettably, the scene abruptly ended after Joshua learned that he was standing on holy ground, leaving us eager future eavesdroppers disappointed. Maybe it was for Joshua's ears only.

Do we have any clues as to the identity of the heavenly captain? A couple of possibilities exist, but certainty is probably beyond our grasp. In Daniel 10, we learned of an angel who had been sent to Daniel in response to prayer. As if apologizing for his tardiness, the heavenly messenger stated, "But the prince of the kingdom of Persia was withstanding me for twenty-one days; then behold, Michael, one of the chief princes, came to help me, for I had been left there with the kings of Persia" (v. 13). Most likely, the angel depicted a skirmish in the spiritual realm to Daniel. No human could possibly delay one of God's mighty angels. Michael came to free the beleaguered angel from this spiritual menace. Interestingly, the Hebrew term for "princes" used to describe Michael's position (v. 13) was the same term that was used in Joshua 5:14 for "captain" (also see Daniel 12:1). We know Michael also had angels in his charge. Revelation 12:7 stated that "Michael and his angels" waged "war" with Satan and his angels. Not to be overlooked, the term *archangel* means "chief angel," and if there is a chief, there must be followers.[92]

> An interesting inference can be drawn from the angel's twenty-one-day delay before visiting Daniel. Angels appear to be bound by time and not omnipresent like God.

Another angel has interesting possibilities as well. Does the angelic captain's request for Joshua to remove his sandals, because he stood on holy ground, ring any bells? When Moses encountered the burning bush on Mount Horeb, Exodus 3:2 indicated that it was the "angel of the LORD" who appeared to Moses in the midst of the bush. Though confusingly, verses 4-5 then stated that "God" called out from the bush and told Moses to remove his sandals because he was on holy ground (you may want to review the section on the angel of the Lord in Chapter 2). Scripture typically referred to places and objects as being holy when associated with God's presence. Because we've noted that the angel of the Lord accepted some accolades that typically were associated with God, it should not surprise us to hear him make the request given to Joshua (Joshua 5:14-15). For the archangel Michael to make such a claim about the place where he stood may have been presumptuous. Although, if he had an exalted position in God's presence on the divine council, perhaps Michael's status was similar to that of the ark of the covenant. His recurrent presence with the Most Holy precipitated his own holiness. Of course, that is just conjecture on my part. The angel of the Lord was seen with a drawn sword on other occasions in Scripture (Numbers 22:23; 1 Chronicles 21:16), which correlates with the captain in Joshua's account (Joshua 5:14-15). We may not be able to pinpoint the identity of the "captain," but we know for certain whose army it was – the Lord's.

One of the most fascinating angel stories in God's Word involved a startling manifestation of the Lord's angelic army. In 2 Kings 6:8-23, we learn that the king of Aram was at war with Israel. Multiple times the prophet Elisha foiled the Aramean king's military strategy by informing the king of Israel of his enemy's plans. Enraged over these repeated failures, the king of Aram accused his confidants that one of them must be a traitor, but one of his servants informed him that Elisha knew even the words the king spoke in the privacy of his own bedroom. Intent on capturing Elisha, the king of Aram deployed by night a battle array of horses, chariots, and infantry to surround the prophet's city of Dothan. As morning dawned, Elisha's servant went outside and saw the Aramean army encircling the city. You can hear the panic in his voice as he asked Elisha, "Alas, my master! What shall we do" (v. 15)? Already at ease with the spiritual realities of the situation, Elisha attempted to calm down his servant:

So he answered, "Do not fear, for those who are with us are more than those who are with them." Then Elisha prayed and said, "O LORD, I pray, open his eyes that he may see." And the LORD opened the servant's eyes, and he saw; and behold, the mountain was full of horses and chariots of fire all around Elisha (vv. 16-17).

Now that's eye opening! Regrettably, the writer did not provide us with the servant's reaction, but what a magnificent sight it must have been to see. The whole mountain must have looked ablaze, because this angelic army outnumbered the "great" army the king of Aram sent to Dothan (v. 14). Confidence and thankfulness surely overwhelmed Elisha's then wide-eyed servant.

Don't we all need an Elisha in our lives? Someone who has a spiritually calming influence because they "know" God is in control. I remember a few years ago sharing with a Navy Chaplain how deeply upset I was with an individual who hindered my progress on a worthy project that I had undertaken. I recall to this very day his cathartic words, "Mike, God's fingerprints are all over this effort. Things will work out; it is the pace of grace my friend." Too stressed out to view the situation with spiritual discernment, this blessed chaplain opened my eyes to God's activity and timing.

What actually were those "horses and chariots of fire?" Were they angels? This was not the first time Elisha caught a glimpse of chariots of fire being mightily drawn by flaming horses. When his mentor Elijah was taken up to heaven by a whirlwind, a "chariot of fire and horses of fire" separated the two (2 Kings 2:11). Elisha shouted out to Elijah, "My father, my father, the chariots of Israel and its horsemen!" (v. 12). Did you observe that Elisha referred to the chariots' "horsemen" in verse 12? They were not initially mentioned in verse 11 as was the case with the chariots and horses of fire on the mountain of Dothan in 2 Kings 16. Therefore, it would be reasonable to assume that angelic horsemen were at the reins ready to guide their chariots into battle against the Arameans as well.

Once the angels came down to Elisha, he prayed to the Lord to strike the Aramean army with blindness. The text conveys that God directly granted Elisha's request. This may lead one to ask, why were these battle-ready angels there to begin with? Besides acting as a source of encouragement, they appear to serve no other purpose in the story. But was this really the case? Is it possible God carried out His will through the angels? We have already shown that God answered prayers through the agency of angels, such as releasing Peter from prison in Acts 12. And the only other place in Scripture where this Hebrew word for blindness was used was in Genesis 19:11, when the angels in Sodom struck the men at Lot's door with blindness.[93] Elisha did not make his request to God until the angels were in his midst (2 Kings 6:18). Present, battle-ready, and armed with the appropriate power, conceivably it was the angels, upon God's command, who struck the bewildered army.

Such sidelights are interesting, but this story holds much broader implications concerning our God. Elisha had the ability to perceive, what appeared to be, dire circumstances through the reality of God's sovereignty.[94] Not relying on his own power, Elisha submitted to the One who controls the outcome of human history.[95] Yes, the story builds confidence in a good outcome because of the angels' presence, but it was the authoritative action of God, instigated by a prayer of faith that brought about the results. Even if it was the angels who struck the Aramean army, it was not an independent act on their part, but the will of their powerful Commander-in-Chief. Power and strength seemed to be on the side of the king of Aram. Weakness appeared to be Elisha's lot. Empowered by His reliance on prayer, Elisha beseeched the almighty King of absolute power, whose will was to deliver His prophet and people from this invading menace.

Who or what do you ultimately have faith in? Probably like many of you, I have some grave concerns about where our country is headed. I recently realized that my primary mode of action was to complain to my congressmen via e-mails. Prayer took on an ancillary role to my pursuit of these politically motivated, spin-master public officials. Duh! As of late, I have turned things around. Prayer to my true King is my primary course of action. I still send my e-mails, but they have already been empowered by prayer. Casting Crowns, a contemporary Christian singing group, recorded the following challenging chorus in their song "What if His People Prayed":

What if His people prayed
And those who bear His name
Would humbly seek His face
And turn from their own way.

The problem comes for us in the fourth line – turning from our own way. Drilled constantly with mottos such as "have it your way" and "you deserve a break," we become believers; "Yeah, that's right I do deserve this or that!" We must admit that it is a struggle in our culture to truly seek God's way in lieu of our own. What great things the church can accomplish through collective, devoted prayer if it comes from hearts that trust in God's sovereign control. Elisha could have sent for the king of Israel to rescue Him, and once the angels saw the Aramean threat, they could have put an end to it on their own. But in both cases, they "knew" God's sovereign will held the optimum solution for the situation.

Jesus offered further insight into the existence of the heavenly army during His arrest. When Peter struck the high priest's slave with a sword, Jesus immediately commanded him to sheath his weapon (John 18:10-11; Matthew 26:51-52). To assure His apostles that He must face what was coming to pass, Jesus asked, "Or do you think that I cannot appeal to My Father, and He will at once put at My disposal more than twelve legions of angels?" (v. 53). Like Elisha, perhaps Jesus saw the

A legion was around 6,000 soldiers, so Jesus stated more than 72,000 angels were at His disposal; a few more than what Ray Overholt suggests in his song "Ten Thousand Angels."

angelic army standing battle-ready on the outskirts of the Garden of Gethsemane to come to His aid. Yet unlike Elisha, Jesus refused to beseech God for help.[96] He knew what was required of Him, and He respected the divine will of His Father.[97] Rescue was not an option, not by the sword of loyal Peter or the strength of twelve dedicated legions of angels. To see mankind treat their Creator (Colossians 1:16) with such wicked disregard, surely made the angelic army a bit edgy, nevertheless they too had to follow the will of the Ruler of the universe. Jesus knew His angelic friends stood ready to help, but His love for mankind paved His way to the cross. With the redemption of mankind at stake, our wonderful Savior unwaveringly proceeded to accomplish His mission.

Even though Jesus did not take advantage of heaven's army at His arrest, He will at His return. John's vision in Revelation 19:11-16 appears to be a reference to the Second Coming, with Jesus portrayed as a conquering warrior, seeking victory over the powers of evil.[98] Jesus has written on His robe and thigh "KING OF KINGS, AND LORD OF LORDS" (v. 16). God has granted Him universal sovereignty as He judges and wages war at the end of the age. With the work of humankind's redemption behind Him, legions of angels are now at Jesus' disposal without constraints. In fact, John states, "And the armies which are in heaven, clothed in fine linen, white and clean, were following Him on white horses" (v. 14). Ready to bring about the full measure of God's righteous kingdom, these heavenly warriors are not arrayed in camouflage fatigues, but laden in white to designate their holiness. This same heavenly force that presumably defeated Satan and his angels under the leadership of Michael, now rides at the pleasure of the warrior-Messiah, ready to wage war with the beast and his army (v. 19).[99] Awaiting a command from their Sovereign Creator, these loyal followers await the final call to battle.

Allegiance and Following

Scripture typically views angels as loyal followers of God and Christ. Of course there have been some exceptions. In Chapter 4, we examined the angels who sinned and were bound and currently await the Final Judgment. I have also mentioned the expulsion of Satan and his angels' from heaven (Revelation 12:7-9). I hope this epic battle will be in God's video library. Satan's specific identity is highly debated and beyond the scope of this book. However, I believe we can safely say that he was a heavenly being of some sort, because he had access to God's presence at one point (Genesis 3:1; Job 1:6-12, 2:1-6; Zechariah 3:1-2). He possibly was a leader in the heavenly realm as he succumbed to the leaders' Achilles heel – pride (1 Timothy 3:6). Whatever the case, Jesus mentioned that eternal fire awaits Satan and his loathsome minions at the Final Judgment (Matthew 25:41).

As God expects the angels to be loyal to Him, He also expects our allegiance as well. We are to know the voice of the great Shepherd and follow Him (John 10:4). Devoted disciples must deny self-rule in order to be considered worthy to follow Jesus' lead (Matthew 16:24). Jesus mentioned that faithfulness was one of the weightier provisions of the Law (23:23). Therefore, following Him is no fair-weather or casual activity. In Hosea 6:4-6, God compared Israel and Judah's loyalty to that of a "morning cloud" and the dew – it was fleeting. Their lack of devotion to Him brought judgments against both nations. God stated, "For I delight in loyalty rather than sacrifice" (v. 6). God primarily desires faithful service and commitment from His people, not pious acts of religion accompanied by a lifestyle where loyalty to Him is shallow at best. Jesus told the persecution-laden church of Smyrna, if they desired to receive "the crown of life," they were to be "faithful until death" (Revelation 2:10).

Being a loyal follower sounds quite daunting, but part of Jesus' ministry was to demonstrate how. No role model can equal our Savior when it comes to loyally following God. Time and again during His earthly ministry, we see Jesus steadfastly seeking to do the will of His Father. We could view the gospel of John as Jesus' treatise on loyalty to God. For Jesus, to accomplish His Father's will was a culinary delight (John 4:34). Loyally serving His Father became the sustenance for producing His spiritual growth. No matter how nutritious our diets might be, nothing can sustain and satisfy our spirit like loyally following and doing the will of our God and Savior. True life springs forth from such devotion and submission.

In 2 Samuel 23:13-17, we are given a story of extreme devotion. David and three of his "mighty men" were trapped by the Philistines in the cave of Adullam. Obsessed by an overwhelming thirst, David innocently vocalized his thoughts; "Oh that someone would give me water to drink from the well of Bethlehem which is by the gate!" (v. 15). Unknown to David, his three valiant warriors broke through the Philistine's lines and secured for their beloved leader his heart's desire. When handed the water, David could not drink it. To him, only the Lord was worthy of the outcome of such a selfless and risk-filled act, so David poured it out as an offering to the Lord. What extraordinary devotion possessed these three men!

Does God deserve devotion of this type? Faced with the fortified walls of our selfish desires, life's temptations, and peer pressures, are we devoted enough to God to spiritually take on such formidable opponents? Jesus expects us to. If we give to those who thirst for a drink, we have done it for Him (Matthew 25:35). In other words, instead of playing golf with friends, if we came to the aid of a heartbroken brother whose wife had just left him – we have given our brother a drink. In so doing, we demonstrated loyalty to the cause of our Lord and quenched His thirst for righteousness.

Satan would love for us to fail at this. In fact, Satan wants us to worship him (Matthew 4:9). He would like to keep us conflicted between two masters, because then we will never show the proper devotion due Christ (6:24). Paul warned that Satan is devious; "But I am afraid that, as the serpent deceived Eve by his craftiness, your minds will be led astray from the simplicity and purity of devotion to Christ" (2 Corinthians 11:3). Our minds and hearts are the battlefield; our eternal destiny the spoils. And to accomplish his mission, Satan can even disguise himself as an angel of light to make his subtle temptations appealing (2 Corinthians

11:14). His servants appear on the scene with righteous "sound-ing" talk (v. 15), hoping to lead us away from the truth. Satan is the "father of lies"; don't ever underestimate him (John 8:44). He wants spiritual death for us. He can make the offerings of this world sound very inviting and appear harmless. Before we know it, another master creeps into our lives and starts to demand our devotion. Divided allegiances never succeed. God has duly warned us. We should search our hearts daily to detect if anything is challenging our loyalty to our universe's Creator and Ruler.

Two thousand years ago, the resurrected Jesus walked with Peter along the shore of the Sea of Galilee to have a heart-to-heart talk with this forthcoming pillar of the church (John 21:19-22). Un-able to stay focused on his own future, Peter suddenly noticed John following them and queried Jesus over John's destiny. Jesus bluntly responded, "[W]hat is that to you? You follow Me!" (v. 22). Perchance Jesus is pleading with you today to reorient your life's direction, "Don't be sidetracked, my beloved disciple, follow Me!"

Guardian Angels?

My oldest sister has slept with a print depicting a guardian angel above her bed throughout most of her life. To this day, she takes great comfort from the message this beautiful piece of art conveys. I must admit, I love that painting as well. With night encroaching and a storm brewing in the distance, a beautiful angel watches over two children as they cross over rushing water on a rickety old bridge. This work of art captures the feelings of many individuals I have be-come acquainted with over the years. They believe a guardian angel watches over them. Even some conservative Christians have shared with me some stories about angels who watched over them that are quite amazing, and who am I to dispute what they have experi-enced? Nevertheless, I would like to examine the concept of whether everyone has an assigned guardian angel in the light of God's Word and His sovereign activity.

A number of passages throughout the Bible make reference to a guarding role performed by some of the angels. In Psalm 91, the

God Himself provides the context for receiving this protection. It is for those who love, know, and call upon Him (Psalm 91:14-15).

psalmist addressed his comforting thoughts to those who take refuge in the Lord and trust in His ability to protect them. God has various schemes at His disposal to look after His people, and the psalmist indicated that one involves the angels; "For He will give His angels charge concerning you, To guard you in all your ways. They will bear you up in their hands, That you do not strike your foot against a stone" (vv. 11-12). During Jesus' encounter with Satan in the wilderness (Matthew 4:5-7), Jesus responded to Satan's inappropriate use of these verses, which has provided us with a commentary on how they should be viewed. With this in mind, James Luther Mays aptly makes the following observation:

> Satan placed Jesus on the pinnacle of the temple and challenged Him to jump off to test God's promise that the angels would bear Him up. The temptation was to take the promised protection of God into the control of his own will and act. That would have shifted the power of the promise from the free sovereignty of God to individual willfulness. Jesus saw that as a way to test God, not as the way of trust. Real trust does not seek to test God or to prove his faithfulness.[100]

Angels are not at our beck and call, but God's. They respond to His commands (or "charge") to watch over His people. Our initiative is to trustingly seek refuge with Him. God's initiative is to faithfully provide protection. And if angels deliver us from harm, it is because of God's sovereign will, not the angels' benevolence.

The Old Testament provides several other examples of angels guarding over God's people. Upon coming out of Egypt, God pledged to aid Israel's conquest of the Promised Land by employing an angel to protect them; "Behold, I am going to send an angel before you to guard you along the way and to bring you into the place which I have prepared" (Exodus 23:20; also see 33:2). In Daniel 12:1, the archangel Michael is referred to as "the great prince who stands guard over the sons of your people." Daniel also mentioned that God sent an angel to protect him when he was cast into the lions' den (Daniel 6:22). David pointed out that a reverential approach to God garners His protection; "The angel of the LORD encamps around those who fear Him, And rescues them" (Psalm 34:7). God, at times, obviously used angelic might to protect and deliver His people.

By using the term "watcher" instead of "angel" in three in-stances (Daniel 4:13, 17, 23), Daniel may have wanted to empha-size their surveillance role over human activities rather than their typical message-bearing responsibilities. In a remarkable vision, Zechariah clearly witnessed the conclusion of an angelic surveil-lance mission (Zechariah 1:7-11). Seeing four angels on horse-back, Zechariah asked the angel who had opened his eyes to the vision, "My lord, what are these?" (v. 9). From the scene of the vi-sion, the angel of the Lord answered him, "These are those whom the LORD has sent to patrol the earth" (v.10). Because they had just completed their reconnaissance mission, the other three an-gels reported their findings to the angel of the Lord: "We have pa-trolled the earth, and behold, all the earth is peaceful and quiet" (v.11). I would like you to observe two things from the vision. The angels were sent by "the LORD," and they "patrolled the earth" (v. 10). The Lord was interested in the status of His creation.

Perhaps the most significant verse in Scripture relating to an-gels watching over humanity came in one of Jesus' discourses to His disciples (Matthew 18:1-14). Jesus set the context for this much-admired verse by pointing out a core trait of a true disciple; one must humble themselves like a child and welcome all such believers. In this passage, it is important to realize that "little ones" (v. 6) is equivalent to Jesus' childlike believers, which hopefully in-cludes you and me. Concerned about others laying stumbling blocks before His precious believers, Jesus stated, "See that you do not despise one of these little ones, for I say to you that their angels in heaven continually behold the face of My Father who is in heaven" (v. 10). Note that this acclaimed verse does not promote the concept that each believer has an assigned angel, but that they have "angels" who are concerned about their well-being. These angels do not act spontaneously, as a direct guardian, but appear to promote our welfare before the throne of God.[101] God may in turn choose to use an angel to minister to us (Hebrews 1:14), but any corresponding action remains with God. I know having an angel we could call our own would be pretty cool, but knowing God cares enough about us to assign angels to report to Him on the well-being of His people is "way cool."

I believe our best course of action is to trust God and place our destiny within His hands, not angels. Shadrach, Meshach, and Abednego provided for us an extreme example of the type of attitude a devoted follower of God should aspire to (Daniel 3). Refusing to worship the gods of the Babylonians during Judah's captivity, this brave trio faced being thrown into a furnace of blazing fire. Standing before King Nebuchadnezzar for judgment, they let the pagan king know their immovable position:

> If it be so, our God whom we serve is able to deliver us from the furnace of blazing fire; and He will deliver us out of your hand, O king. But even if He does not, let it be known to you, O king, that we are not going to serve your gods or worship the golden image that you have set up (vv. 17-18).

Wouldn't it be great to have an ounce of that type of faith? Enraged, the king wasted no time in having the faithful threesome tied up and tossed into the raging furnace. Encountering such intense heat, the men who threw the three into the furnace were immediately consumed. Unable to fathom what he then saw, Nebuchadnezzar shockingly exclaimed, "Look! I see four men loosed and walking about in the midst of the fire without harm, and the appearance of the fourth is like the son of the gods!" (v. 25). After the king commanded the fortunate trio to come out, all present noticed that the fire had no effect on them. Not even one hair on their head was singed nor did they smell of smoke. Have you ever put a hair in a flame and watch it shrink into a little ball? If the flames had any effect on their hair, imagine their resulting hairdos. The trio's trust was well placed. What a dramatic rescue! What an amazing power this angel possessed. Well before humankind invented the Space Shuttle's heat-resistant tiles, the angels apparently possessed this technology as standard equipment.

We may never be able to understand why God chooses a particular course of action in this life, but we must trust His ability to work out all things for good for those who love Him. We might ask, why did God make Shadrach, Meshach, and Abednego go through such a horrible ordeal? Why not rescue them earlier, so they could have avoided such a terror-filled trial? Look at the conclusion of the story:

> Nebuchadnezzar responded and said, "Blessed be the God of Shadrach, Meshach and Abed-nego, who has sent His angel and delivered His servants who put their trust in Him, violating the king's command, and yielded up their bodies so as not to serve or worship any god except their own God" (Daniel 3:28)

Before many of his royal subjects, this pagan king blessed God and went on to decree that the people of Babylon should hold the Lord in high esteem. Not an ending I would have predicted. God works things out according to His good purposes. Our Lord and God reigns! Angels bow to His sovereignty. How about you?

Questions

1. How important do you think it is to have a vision for the future laid out before us? Why is this important? What vision has God given to us?

2. What does God's Word inform us about the position of angels relative to God? What commonly-believed descriptions of an angel's physical appearance are not supported by Scripture?

3. Why would God have an angelic army? What conclusions can we draw from this?

4. What precipitated God's action in the Elisha story? Why do you think the angels were present?

5. With the Aramean army ready to cause him harm, Elisha's spiritual insight allowed him to view the situation through the reality of God's sovereignty. What effect did that have on him; on his servant? How can viewing our daily circumstances through God's sovereignty aid our Christian walk? What stands in our way of achieving this?

6. What does God expect from us regarding our loyalty to Him? How can our devotion to God become divided? Why should that be a concern to us?

7. How does Satan attempt to confound our allegiance to God? Give some practical examples in your life on how this might occur.

8. Does Scripture teach that each of us have an assigned guardian angel? Have angels had a role in guarding God's people throughout history? What does Scripture teach as to the interaction between God, the angels, and His people in accomplishing this protective function?

9. Should Christians place their trust in angels? If not, where should they place it? Give some examples of aspects of your life where you need to place more trust in God.

Chapter 11

Crucifixion, Resurrection, and Enthronement

But of the Son He says, "Your throne, O God,
is forever and ever, And the righteous scepter
is the scepter of His kingdom (Hebrews 1:8).

You will find this chapter a little different than the rest. To provide an angelic perspective, I have put together a potential scenario of the heavenly hosts' activity around the time of Jesus' crucifixion, resurrection, and enthronement. Thanks for allowing me to indulge into this fictional exercise that uses scriptural fact as its framework. Before proceeding to the scene of the crucifixion, let's explore a contemporary story of human tragedy.

Challenger's Final Countdown

Prior to walking into the Launch Control Center at the Kennedy Space Center in the early morning hours of January 28, 1986, I stopped and viewed the Space Shuttle Challenger perched on her launch pad three and one-half miles away. What a beautiful sight it was to see her all lit up by the xenon lights – a true technological wonder. As usual, she beckoned me to be ever vigilant in the coming hours; and, as always, I was willing to comply. Little did I know that before this day closed my life would be forever changed by Challenger's ill-fated destiny.

An unfamiliar bitter cold had gripped this area of Florida. To escape the uncomfortable temperature, I hurried into the warmth of the Launch Control Center. After entering Firing Room 3, I made my way back to the Space Shuttle Main Engine Avionics console to join my contractor counterparts. The Challenger's countdown had been underway for a couple of days, and we were preparing her for launch later that morning. The critical operation of loading cryogenic propellants into the Shuttle's External Tank was the next major task, and it was my turn to support this important event. During the tanking process, super cold cryogenic fluids are also introduced into the main engines. Because my system monitored the health of the engines, our role was to be especially attentive for anomalies as these super cold liquids thermally shock the engines' lines, valves, and turbo-machinery. Vulnerability to serious hazards, especially leaks, increases during this time frame.

In the launch business, boring countdowns are what you hope for. A number of problems can cause a launch to be scrubbed, so a great deal of unplanned activity in the Firing Room is a bad omen. My colleagues and I felt fortunate that morning because our system performed beautifully. Others though had serious difficulties to deal with. A number of engineers diligently worked on issues related to the cold temperatures. One of the more prominent problems involved the formation of icicles on the launch tower. To protect the launch pad water lines, the water system had been configured to allow the water to slowly flow out and into the drains. Unexpectedly, ice formed over the drains, and the high winds had spread the water around the structure. Ice on the launch tower could turn into a potential debris concern during the initial phase of the launch. If a piece of ice came loose and ricocheted off the structure and struck the Shuttle's fragile heat protection tile, the resulting damage could be a concern for the entry phase of the mission. So a special team went out to the launch pad to assess the problem and take the appropriate action.[102] But at my console, the morning continued to be fairly mundane. The lack of activity made us especially aware of the frigid temperature in the Firing Room. The cold weather outside had made the usual chilly environment of the Firing Room even worse. It felt like they had mistakenly pumped the cryogenic fluids directly into the Launch Control Center.

When the launch team reported for duty, those of us who had supported the tanking were released. Of the twenty-four launches to date, I supported all but a few of them from either the primary or management Firing Rooms. However, for those remaining few, I stayed and watched the launch from outside the Launch Control Center. As you might imagine, viewing a launch in such close proximity was a great perk for those of us on the tanking team. Nevertheless, after working all night, I was exhausted and decided to head home. I would have to battle the tourist traffic after the liftoff if I stayed. You would be amazed at the amount of people that invade the Space Coast to watch a launch. I don't blame them – it's pretty special. So for the first time, I planned to catch the final stages of the countdown on television, run outside and watch the Shuttle's ascent from my front yard, and then afterward take my sleep-deprived body straight to bed.

Sticking to my plan, as soon as I saw ignition and the Shuttle clear the launch tower from the comfort of my living room, I bolted outside. Even from my home in Titusville, the sight was spectacular. I participated in a great deal of ascent simulations during my career, so I intimately knew the flight profile. I remember thinking it was about time for the Challenger to be coming out of the region of maximum dynamic pressure, so the flight computers would be throttling the main engines back up to 104 percent thrust, when all of a sudden an immense cloud appeared. I could hardly believe my eyes. I knew something had gone horribly wrong, yet hope against hope led me to believe that one of the abort modes might still be achievable.

In a Return to Launch Site abort, the vehicle keeps heading downrange, separates the spent Solid Rocket Boosters, and eventually pitches 180 degrees around and heads back toward KSC.

After shutting down the engines and ditching the tank in the ocean, the Orbiter glides back and lands on the Shuttle runway at KSC. So hoping this sporty abort was still possible, I ran back inside to observe the view from the tracking cameras on television and at once noticed the boosters aimlessly propelling themselves across the sky. Frantically, I repeated over and over, "Where is the Orbiter, where is the Orbiter?" A Return to Launch Site abort was no longer possible, and no other abort modes remained for this phase of the mission. Then I heard the Mission Control Center's spokesman state, "Flight controllers here are looking very carefully at the situation. Obviously, a major malfunction."

My soul felt like it had been torn in two. I jumped into my car and headed back to KSC. I did not know what I would do when I arrived, but I knew that KSC is where I needed to be. What a horrible drive! Emotions seemed to come and go. One minute I frantically searched the radio for news; then tears started to flow. I began to talk to myself out loud as I tried to evaluate what happened. My mind was on autopilot as I drove, and thank God for allowing me to make it to my office in one piece.

As I hurried into our office building, I found everyone stricken with an overwhelming array of thoughts and emotions. Many of us had worked directly with the Challenger crew and to think that they were no longer with us was unimaginable. Why? was not the predominant question. Each person seemed to be asking whether they somehow contributed to this horrible accident. Because I worked on the Space Shuttle Main Engines, I knew they could have easily played a part in the catastrophe. And to think what the

Challenger carried a privileged passenger aboard. Christa McAuliffe was the first recipient of the Teacher in Space Program and was destined to become the first teacher in space. Tragically, thousands of children from across our nation watched in dismay as the explosion took the life of this hero from the classroom.

families of the flight crew witnessed and were going through – it was nothing short of heartrending. In the back of our minds we also thought, what would become of the Space Shuttle program? Tears and fears rocked our very souls. Engulfed in helplessness, the unthinkable invaded our world.

Haunted by the images of the explosion, falling debris, and the boosters aimlessly traversing the sky, we tried to find consoling words for one another, but nothing could penetrate the unrelenting shock of the tragedy. The last words of the Challenger's Commander, Dick Scobee, still echoed in our heads; "Roger, go at throttle up," with the accompanying crackle that abruptly ended the communication. We tried to make sense of it all, but many days would have to pass before a definite explanation would be developed.

Later that day we were asked to gather in Firing Room 3, where the Challenger had been launched. Vice President George Bush and Senators John Glenn and Jake Garn were flying from Washington D.C. to meet with us.[103] They carried a message of hope from President Reagan and their own hearts. Vice President Bush tearfully spoke of the Challenger's crew and families, and then gave us a message of reassurance. He assured us that the Space Program would persevere. We would find the problems and fix them. Of course we knew that, but in our frail state, hearing these words directly from the vice president had a rallying affect on our beleaguered spirits. Prefaced by extreme devotion, undue diligence, and technical excellence, Shuttles would once again rise up from the Kennedy Space Center.

Crucifixion

A little less than two thousand years before the Challenger accident, around A.D. 33, another dark and tragic day intruded on our world. Renounced by the Jewish religious elite, our Lord and Savior was handed over to the pagan Romans and crucified. From the title of Max Lucado's book, *And the Angels Were Silent*, one must reflect on the lack of angelic activity during the final hours of Jesus' life.

Angels had announced Mary's pregnancy and Jesus' birth, warned Joseph of Herod's death plot against Jesus, attended to Jesus in the wilderness, comforted Him in the Garden of Gethsemane, announced His resurrection, and witnessed His ascension. But where were the angels during Jesus' arrest, trial, and crucifixion?

No doubt, the angels intently watched God's plan unfolding. In the hours prior to Jesus' arrest, they might have noted a sense of melancholy in Jesus' voice, but they probably wondered, "Why does He keep insinuating He would soon be departing?" For example, when He taught the apostles to "love one another," Jesus mentioned, "I am with you a little while longer" (John 13:33-34). Jesus told the apostles that He was leaving so He could "prepare a place" for them in His "Father's house" (14:2). Even though the apostles' hearts were filled with sorrow, Jesus told them that His departure would be to their advantage, because He would send them the Holy Spirit (16:5-7). And after instituting the Lord's Supper, Jesus said, "I will not drink of this fruit of the vine from now on until that day when I drink it new with you in My Father's kingdom" (Matthew 26:29).

God's vigilant angels surely knew something was awry. They were undoubtedly concerned when Satan tempted Judas to betray Jesus (John 13:2). But when Satan actually entered this traitorous apostle, the angels probably went on red alert. Jesus knew what was occurring spiritually, and He told Judas, "What you do, do quickly" (v. 27).

From our investigation of guardian angels, Daniel stated that the archangel Michael watched over God's people (Daniel 12:1), and I think Jesus qualified in that regard. We also learned that believers were not to be "despised" because "their angels" have an audience with God in heaven (Matthew 18:10). It would be safe to assume that Jesus held believer status as well, so "silence" may not be the appropriate word, even rhetorically, to describe the angels' activity. Anxiously, they probably went before God's throne on numerous occasions. Observing Jesus' betrayal and arrest, a mockery of a trial, the utter cruelty inflicted upon Jesus, and ultimately the crucifixion, assuredly drove the bewildered angels to their knees before God. Their Creator was being mocked, scourged, spat upon, and unbelievably sentenced to death. Endowed with tremendous power, God's heavenly hosts surely pleaded with the Almighty to cut them loose on a rescue mission.

Each time God's beloved angels came before Him, His answer would have been "no." With an understanding and confident tone, He must have assured them that what was transpiring had to take place. The redemption of humanity was unfolding before the angels' eyes, yet what it entailed was hard to behold.

Restrained and out of their control, the obedient angels looked on as Jesus was crucified. Golgotha may have been ablaze with their spiritual presence, but they stood virtually powerless because of their steadfast adherence to God's will. Echoes of Roman hammers clanging against the spikes rang through the heavenly realm as they tore through the bone and flesh of the innocent Son of God. Daniel's title for the angels seems most appropriate at this scene, because all the "watchers" could do was watch. When Jesus cried out to His Father, "My God, My God, why have You forsaken Me?" (Matthew 27:46), the angels might have thought, "Certainly, orders from the Most High are coming!" But only moments later, their Creator, Leader, and friend cried out again with a loud voice, and "yielded up His spirit" (v. 50). The unthinkable happened – Jesus was dead.

These emotionally charged beings shouted with joy when God created the earth (Job 38:7). They join God with great joy when a believer repents and returns to Him (Luke 15:10). Surely they were acquainted with sorrow. Some of their comrades fell ages ago, and God's people often detrimentally strayed from their gracious God. I wonder – do you think angels cry? If they do, teardrops may have filled those streets of gold like confetti falling at a ticker tape parade. I am sure they wondered what good could come out of such tragedy.

Return to Flight

Two years and eight months passed, and the Firing Room again hosted a group of hopeful and devoted engineers, ready to launch the Space Shuttle Discovery. After much analysis, many safety modifications, and tighter launch constraints, Discovery was prepared to grace the Florida skies with her power and beauty. During the final stages of a countdown, a feeling of excitement typically comes over the launch team as the clock counts down – 10, 9, 8 ... , but not that time. Pins and needles suddenly replaced the comfort of our cushioned seats on this nerve-racking occasion. The changes made to the Shuttles gave us the confidence the vehicles were ready to fly again, but visions of the Challenger exploding could not be suppressed. Space flight is a dangerous business.

As three million pounds of thrust lifted Discovery off her pad, its powerful acoustic shock waves once again shook the Space Coast. Not only had I prayed fervently that morning for a safe mission, but prayers silently came forth as I knew all was beyond our control.

The tension mounted when the Shuttle went through the region of maximum dynamic pressure, and it was almost unbearable as we watched the engines throttle up. When the commander of Discovery said, "Roger, go at throttle up," and the Shuttle made it past the point of the Challenger accident, some relief started to set in. But until the main engines shut down, the pins and needles would relentlessly persist.

After two minutes into the flight, the Solid Rocket Boosters separated, and cheers of joy immediately went up in the Firing Room. But they became quickly muted as the main engines still had six and half minutes of burn time remaining, and everyone knew the serious nature of these intense minutes. At about eight and half minutes into the flight, I saw the main engines starting their shutdown sequence, and then the Flight Director announced, "We have MECO" (MECO is an acronym for main engine cutoff). Shouts of joy, like you wouldn't believe, erupted from these normally subdued engineers. Tears uncontrollably rolled down our cheeks as hugs, high fives, pats on the back, and hardy hand-shakes were being exchanged. We had done it! We successfully returned to flight the Shuttle fleet.

Resurrection

Early in the morning on the third day after Jesus' death, one of God's faithful angels was summoned to the throne room. With the recent horrible turn of events, he did not know what to expect, but a glorious assignment awaited him. God informed the angel that He had just resurrected His beloved Son. The angel's mission was to enter the earthly realm and open Jesus' tomb to reveal that humanity's Savior had risen from the grave. Just to be selected to take on such a wonderful mission was exciting enough; but fueled by the additional news that Jesus lived, the angel probably could hardly contain himself! It was time to let his light shine. Matthew shared an interesting insight as this privileged angel carried out his mission:

> And behold, a severe earthquake had occurred, for an angel of the Lord descended from heaven and came and rolled away the stone and sat upon it. And his appearance was like lightning, and his clothing as white as snow (Matthew 28:2-3).

This angel did not subtly slip into the physical realm like his heavenly cohorts only to startle some unsuspecting human because of his sudden appearance. Revealing God's power in the resurrection of Jesus demanded an earth-shattering entrance, so this joyous angel's descent into the physical realm came with such a burst of energy that a "severe" earthquake occurred. After rolling away the stone with his angelic might, the angel triumphantly sat on it. Coming to the tomb to anoint Jesus' body with spices, Mary Magdalene and Mary, the mother of James, were overcome with fear at the sight of this supernatural visitor. Even so, the angel's posture must have invitingly communicated,

"Come, behold what the Almighty has done!" because he immediately enticed the women to share in his good news by verifying that Christ was no longer confined to the grave.

> Do not be afraid; for I know that you are looking for Jesus who has been crucified. He is not here, for He has risen, just as He said. Come, see the place where He was lying (Matthew 28:5-6).

What an honor to make this blessed announcement, "He is not here, for He has risen" (v. 6). Because the extreme significance of this proclamation, one might have expected to hear God's voice thundering out of heaven to declare this wonderful news, similar as to when He called out at Jesus' baptism: "This is My beloved Son, in whom I am well-pleased" (3:17). Yet God decided to reward a devoted member of the heavenly ranks to deliver this momentous message. What joy and what excitement this angel undoubtedly experienced!

In the Greek, the phrase "He has risen" is in the passive voice. Jesus did not raise Himself; it was through the power of God.[104]

What do you think, do angels hug? Phenomenal rejoicing had to embrace all of heaven as the news spread that Jesus was alive. Over the centuries, the angels probably never became accustomed to the shocking achievements brought about by their almighty Lord, but resurrecting Jesus to eternal life surely astounded these heavenly spectators. What a tremendous swing in emotions the angels experienced. Still dealing with the grief of losing the Son of God, they suddenly encountered the joy, excitement, and amazement of the news that Jesus lives, JESUS LIVES! Only one response could follow, tears again rained down in heaven.

The Christian Hope

Angels are undoubtedly incredible creatures. They can accomplish many astonishing things, such as causing earthquakes, blinding oppressors, shutting the mouths of lions, and talking to humans in their dreams. Whereas humankind is extraordinarily innovative, for example advancing surgical procedures to be less invasive, developing technology to enhance the quality of life, providing the ability to view vast amounts of information over the Internet, and even achieving space flight. However, only God has the power to resurrect a human life to spend eternity with Him in heaven.

Where do we place our hope? Political figures may promise us the world, but I think you would agree with me that their promises frequently go unfulfilled and are often empty rhetoric. At times, we can rely on our innovativeness to work through life's problems, but sometimes solutions don't come so easily, if at all. The design of a Space Shuttle was a remarkable achievement, but we have seen its limitations in the Challenger and Columbia disasters. Angels also have their constraints and are just devoted servants of God created to accomplish His purposes. So why does humanity so often place their hopes on individuals and things that may lack the ability to fulfill them? Is God not the source of true hope? His love for humanity is grounded in the cross, and Jesus' resurrection demonstrates His ability to deliver on the promise of eternal life to His faithful. God's character is proven, His creative power is unparalleled. When He promises us something, it is not empty rhetoric; He has the power to deliver. As Peter eloquently proclaimed, God mercifully offers us the ability "to be born again to a living hope through the resurrection of Jesus Christ from the dead" (1 Peter 1:3). A hope that does not disappoint!

Enthronement

Picture the joyous celebration that must have accompanied Jesus' entrance into the throne room after His ascension. Around the crystal sea that surrounds God's throne, myriads and myriads of angels pressed in tightly together, watching in awe as the Son approached His Father's throne. Consistent with His humble nature, I imagine Jesus would have bowed before His Father and proudly stated, "Mission accomplished! Your glorious will has been done." While God placed a crown upon His Son's head, the angels humbly and reverently bowed in recognition of their new King. But when God turned to His heavenly hosts and introduced King Jesus, a worshipful celebration must have commenced. I would venture to guess that the angels wished they did have halos, so they could have tossed them in the air like elated new graduates fling their graduation caps. What a monumental day in heaven – a day the angels will never forget.

Thirty-three years earlier the angel Gabriel prophesied to Mary of her future Son's kingly status.

> He will be great, and will be called the Son of the Most High; and the Lord God will give Him the throne of His father David; and He will reign over the house of Jacob forever; and His kingdom will have no end (Luke 1:32-33).

With Gabriel's prophecy fulfilled at Jesus' enthronement at the right hand of God, we now live under the rule of our Savior. Is your view of Jesus totally complete? Does Jesus reign in your life? Isn't it time that you join the angels with a heartfelt exclamation that drives you to your knees, that Jesus reigns? JESUS REIGNS!

Summary

We easily become attracted to the mysterious, and Scripture certainly presents the angels in such a fashion. But angels are not interested in us becoming enthralled with them. I hope our investigation in this book has revealed to you just the contrary. Angels want you to become enthralled with God and Jesus. Angels in God's Word serve to draw us to Him; they point away from themselves. Their firsthand experience with God exposes us to His exalted nature, and how we should respond to Him. I hope through the pages of this book you have encountered, and will continue to encounter, God in a new and spiritually-rich way. As co-servants to our Creator, let's join the angels in adoration and service to our wonderful Lord and God.

Questions

1. Have you ever experienced a life tragedy where you felt totally helpless? Can any good come from such life experiences? Explain.

2. Why do you think the angels did not intervene during Jesus' arrest, trial, and crucifixion? What do you think they were doing? What might have been their concerns? From all this, what insight should we gain?

3. Have you ever experienced so much joy that you could not control your tears? When you read the words "He is not here, for He has risen," how does that make you feel? How do you want them to make you feel?

4. Do you think the angel of Matthew 28:2 was excited about his assigned mission? What supports your belief?

5. Where do we often place our hopes? What are some of the reasons that we should place our hope in God? Have you?

6. Does Jesus truly reign in your life? If not, what actions do you need to take to allow this to occur?

7. How have the stories of the angels allowed you to encounter God in new ways? How might your approach to God be different in the future?

Endnotes

Chapter 1

1   All biblical references in this book are taken from *The Hebrew-Greek Key Study Bible: New American Standard Bible*. Chattanooga: AMG Publishers, 1990.

2   Baylor University. *The Baylor Religion Survey* (Waco, TX: Baylor Institute for Studies of Religion, 2005).

3   Ibid.

4   Karl Barth, *Church Dogmatics*, ed. G. W. Bromiley and T. F. Torrance, vol. 3, pt. 3, *The Doctrine of Creation*, trans. G. W. Bromiley and R. J. Ehrlich (Edinburgh: T. & T. Clark, 1960), 514.

5   Duane A. Garrett, *Angels and the New Spirituality* (Nashville: Broadman & Holman, 1995), 237.

6   George Howe Colt, "In Search of Angels," *Life*, December 1995, 74.

7   Nancy Gibbs, "Angels Among Us," *Time*, 27 December 1993, 65.

8   Hilda Kuester, "Looking for Angels," *Christian Ministry* 26 (May-June 1995): 9.

Chapter 2

[9]   Victor Knowles, *Angels and Demons: Agents of God & Satan* ...
      A Biblical Study (Joplin, MO: College Press, 1994), 47.

[10] Wynelle F. Main, *An Investigation of Angels* (Abilene, TX: Qual-
      ity Publications), 103.

[11] Ibid.

Holiness Prelude

[12] Millard J. Erickson, *Christian Theology*, 2^d ed. (Grand Rapids:
      Baker Academic), 311.

[13] L. Berkhof, *Systematic Theology*, 4th ed. (Grand Rapids: Eerd-
      mans), 73.

[14] Erickson, *Christian Theology*, 311.

[15] John M. Frame, *The Doctrine of God* (Memphis, TN: P&R Pub-
      lishing, 2002), 27.

Chapter 3

[16] William Reynolds, *The Private Journal of William Reynolds:
      United States Exploring Expedition, 1838-1842* (New York: Pen-
      guin Books, 2004), 45.

[17] "Friends, Family, the Nation Honor Fallen Columbia Astro-
      nauts; Investigators Focus on Possible Damage to Shuttle at
      Takeoff," *CNN Connie Chung Tonight* (4 Feb. 2003) [on-line

transcript]; http://transcripts.cnn.com/TRANSCRIPTS/0302/ 04/cct.00.html; Internet; accessed 18 August 2005.

18   John N. Oswalt, *The Book of Isaiah: Chapters 1-39*, The New International Commentary on the Old Testament, (Grand Rapids: Eerdmans, 1986), 178-79.

19   Ibid., 179.

20   George Buchanan Gray, *A Critical and Exegetical Commentary on the Book of Isaiah*, The International Critical Commentary, (Edinburgh: T&T Clark, 1912), 1:104-105.

21   Ancient Near Eastern literature often used the Hebrew term translated "feet" as a euphemism for genitalia. If this is the case then two wings are used to cover the seraphim's nakedness, which also would be an act of humility in the presence of the Creator. Reference Oswalt, *The Book of Isaiah*, 179.

22   Otto Kaiser, *Isaiah 1-12*, The Old Testament Library, (Philadelphia: Westminster, 1983), 126.

23   Thomas G. Smothers, "A Superior Model: Hebrews 1:1-4:13," *Review & Expositor* 82 (Summer 1985): 334-35.

24   Neil R. Lightfoot, *Jesus Christ Today: A Commentary on the Book of Hebrews* (Grand Rapids: Baker, 1976), 38.

25   For a discussion of apocalyptic angelology and how it influenced Judaism see J. Daryl Charles, "The Angels, Sonship and Birthright in the Letter to the Hebrews," *Journal of the Evangelical Theological Society* 33 (June 1990): 172-74.

26 Robert H. Mounce, *The Book of Revelation*, The New International Commentary on the New Testament, (Grand Rapids: Eerdmans, 1997), 121.

27 *Millennial Harbinger*, May 1843.

28 John B. Dykes, "Holy, Holy, Holy," words by Reginald Heber.

Chapter 4

29 C. Fred Dickason, *Angels Elect & Evil* (Chicago: Moody Press, 1975), 66.

30 For support of "sons of God" referring to lineage of Seth see Kenneth A. Mathews, *Genesis 1-11:26*, The New American Commentary, vol. 1A (Nashville, TN: Broadman & Holman, 2002), 329-32.

31 The specific references for these documents are 1 Enoch 6-22; 2 Bar. 56:10-14; Jub. 4:22-23 and 5:1-2; T. of Reu. 5:6-7; T. of Naph. 3:5; CD 2:17-19; Philo, *On the Giants*; Josephus, *Ant.* 1.3.1; 1QaGen 2:1; *The Book of Giants* fragments from 1Q23, 4Q530 4Q531, 4Q532.

32 James H. Charlesworth, *The Old Testament Pseudepigrapha*, vol. 1 (Garden City, NY: 1983), 21.

33 Ibid., 20.

34 James H. Charlesworth, *The Old Testament Pseudepigrapha*, vol. 2 (Garden City, NY: 1983), 64.

35 Charlesworth, *The Old Testament Pseudepigrapha*, vol. 1, 784.

36 Ibid., 641.

37 Josephus, *Josephus: Complete Works*, trans. by William Whitson (Grand Rapids: Kregel, 1960), 28.

38 Thomas R. Schreiner, *1, 2 Peter, Jude*, The New American Commentary, vol. 37 (Nashville, TN: Broadman & Holman, 2003), 451.

39 Roy Ratcliff, *Dark Journey Deep Grace: Jeffrey Dahmer's Story of Faith* (Abilene, TX: Leafwood, 2006).

Love Prelude

40 Erickson, *Christian Theology*, 318.

41 Ibid., 321.

42 Berkhof, *Systematic Theology*, 72.

43 Jack Cottrell, *What the Bible Says About God the Redeemer* (Joplin, MO: College Press, 1987), 353.

Chapter 5

44 Barth, *Church Dogmatics*, vol. 3, pt. 3, 496.

45 D. A. Carson, "Matthew," in *The Expositor's Bible Commentary*, ed. Frank E. Gaebelein (Grand Rapids: Zondervan, 1984), 8:76.

46 Edward P. Myers, *Angelology: A Study of Angels* (West Monroe, LA: Howard, 1990), 40.

[47]   I. Howard Marshall, *The Acts of the Apostles: An Introduction and Commentary*, The Tyndale New Testament Commentaries, vol. 5 (Grand Rapids: Eerdmans, 1980), 161.

[48]   For this opinion refer to Travis L. Quertermous, *The Hosts of Heaven: A Biblical Study of Angels*, (Henderson, TN: Hester Publications, 2002), 197; and Knowles, *Angels and Demons*, 79.

[49]   John Murray, *The Epistle to the Romans*, The New International Commentary on the New Testament, (Grand Rapids: Eerdmans, 1968), 333.

[50]   For a good discussion of these terms and probable meanings refer to Murray, *The Epistle to the Romans*, 332-33.

Chapter 6

[51]   Robert Davidson, *Genesis 12-50*, The Cambridge Bible Commentary, (London: Cambridge University Press, 1979), 52.

[52]   Iain W. Provan, *1 and 2 Kings*, New International Bible Commentary, (Peabody, Massachusetts: Hendrickson Publishers, 1995), 144.

[53]   Quertermous, *The Hosts of Heaven*, 115.

[54]   Carson, "Matthew," 543.

[55]   A. C. Gaebelein, *What the Bible Says About Angels* (Grand Rapids: Baker Book House, 1987), 70.

[56] Stephen F. Noll, *Angels of Light, Powers of Darkness: Thinking Biblically about Angels, Satan & Principalities* (Downers Grove, IL: InterVarsity Press, 1998), 78.

[57] Barth, *Church Dogmatics*, vol. 3, pt. 3, 501.

Chapter 7

[58] James B. Irwin, *To Rule the Night: The Discovery Voyage of Astronaut Jim Irwin* (Philadelphia: A. J. Holman, 1973), 19.

[59] Ibid.

[60] Walter Bauer, *A Greek-English Lexicon of the New Testament and Other Early Christian Literature*, 3rd ed., rev. and ed. Frederick William Danker (Chicago: University of Chicago Press, 2000), 1001 (Hereafter referred as *BDAG*).

[61] M. Robert Mulholland, *Invitation to a Journey: A Road Map for Spiritual Formation* (Downers Grove, IL: InterVarsity Press, 1993), 37-38.

[62] Norman W. Porteous, *Daniel: A Commentary*, The Old Testament Library, (Philadelphia: Westminster Press, 1965), 139.

[63] Stephen R. Miller, *Daniel*, The New American Commentary, vol. 18 (Nashville: Broadman & Holman, 1994), 250.

[64] Ibid., 251-52.

Justice Prelude

[65] Cottrell, *God the Redeemer*, 236.

[66]   Frame, *The Doctrine of God*, 456.

[67]   Ibid.

[68]   Cottrell, *God the Redeemer*, 216.

[69]   Erickson, *Christian Theology*, 315.

[70]   Ibid.

Chapter 8

[71]   H. Wheeler Robinson, "The Council of Yahweh," *Journal of Theological Studies* 45 (1944): 152.

[72]   Dickason, *Angels Elect & Evil*, 86.

[73]   Gerald Cooke, "The Sons of (the) God(s)," in *Zeitschrift Fur Die Alttestamentliche Wisseschaft*, ed. Georg Fohrer, Otto Eibfeldt and Johannes Hempel (Berlin: Verlag Von Alfred Topelmann, 1964), 7:36.

[74]   Marvin H. Pope, *Job*, The Anchor Bible, vol. 15 (Garden City, NY: Doubleday, 1965), 9. Also see Norman C. Habel, *The Book of Job*, The Old Testament Library, (Philadelphia: Westminster Press, 1985), 89.

[75]   R. W. L. Moberly, "Does God Lie to His Prophets? The Story of Micaiah ben Imlah as a Test Case," *Havard Theological Review* 96 (January 2003): 6 [journal on-line]; available from Wilson-Select through OCLC FirstSearch http://newfirstsearch. oclc.org; Internet; accessed on 10 April 2006.

[76] George M. Landes, "Shall We Neglect the Angels?" *Union Seminary Quarterly Review* 14 (May 1959): 23.

Chapter 9

[77] Gerhard Von Rad, *Genesis: A Commentary*, The Old Testament Library, (Philadelphia: Cambridge Westminster Press, 1961), 206.

[78] E. A. Speiser, *Genesis*, The Anchor Bible, vol. 1 (New York: Doubleday, 1964), 139.

[79] Richard D. Nelson, *First and Second Kings*, Interpretation, (Louisville: John Knox Press, 1987), 240-41.

[80] Josephus, *Antiquities of the Jews* 19.18.2.

[81] Darrell L. Bock, *Acts*, Baker Exegetical Commentary on the New Testament (Grand Rapids: Baker Academic, 2007), 431-32.

[82] Josephus, *Antiquities of the Jews* 19.18.2.

[83] Ibid.

Sovereignty Prelude

[84] Mulholland, *Invitation to a Journey*, 26.

[85] Jack Cottrell, *What the Bible Says About God the Ruler* (Eugene, Oregon: Wipf & Stock, 1984), 266.

86 Robert P. Lightner, *Evangelical Theology: A Survey and Review* (Grand Rapids: Baker Book House, 1986), 54.

87 Barth, *Church Dogmatics*, vol. 2, pt. 1, 301.

Chapter 10

88 Evelyn Husband, *High Calling: The Courageous Life and Faith of Space Shuttle Columbia Commander Rick Husband* (Nashville: Thomas Nelson, 2003), 115.

89 James L. Mays, *Psalms*, Interpretation, (Louisville: John Knox Press, 1994), 445.

90 Ibid., 284.

91 Kaiser, *Isaiah 1-12*, 126.

92 *BDAG*, 137.

93 John Gray, *I & II Kings: A Commentary*, The Old Testament Library, (Philadelphia: Westminster Press, 1975), 517.

94 Walter Brueggemann, "The Embarrassing Footnote," *Theology Today* 44 (April 1987): 9.

95 Ibid.

96 Carson, "Matthew," 548.

97 Craig L. Blomberg, *Matthew*, New American Commentary, vol. 22 (Nashville: Broadman, 1992), 399.

98   George Eldon Ladd, *A Commentary on the Revelation of John* (Grand Rapids: Eerdmans, 1972), 252.

99   David E. Aune, *Revelation 17-22*, Word Biblical Commentary, vol. 52C (Nashville: Thomas Nelson, 1998), 1059.

100 Mays, *Psalms*, 298.

101 Donald A. Hagner, *Matthew 14-28*, Word Biblical Commentary, vol, 33B (Nashville, TN: Nelson, 1995), 527.

Chapter 11

102 James A. Thomas, *Some Trust in Chariots: The Space Shuttle Challenger Experience* (Longwood, FL: Xulon Press, 2006), 178.

103 Ibid., 218.

104 Blomberg, *Matthew*, 427.

Endorsements for *An Angel's View*

This is not your commonplace angel book. We were impressed with O'Neal's fresh insights into the complex character of God. His nature is revealed through the perspective of those who know him best.... those who live with him....the angels.   What a great idea and what a wonderful book.

Charlie & Gayle Griffin, Titusville, FL

Mike provides a unique, encouraging, and often challenging glimpse behind the scenes of this physical world into the heavenly realms where we witness the glory of God through the ministry of angels. I was blessed to revisit some of the greatest moments of history from an entirely new perspective.

Scott Laird, Pulpit Minister, Great Falls, MT

CPSIA information can be obtained
at www.ICGtesting.com
Printed in the USA
BVHW03101924121
624760BV000006B/333